Editors

C. C. Lamberg-Karlovsky

Jeremy A. Sabloff

Harvard University

PREHISTORIC CARRYING CAPACITY: A MODEL

Ezra B. W. Zubrow
Stanford University

Cummings Publishing Company
Menlo Park, California ▲▲▼

ISBN: 0-8465-8779-3

ABCDEFGHIJKL-AL-7987654

Cummings Publishing Company, Inc.
2727 Sand Hill Road
Menlo Park, California   94025

In Memorium
Edward P. Dozier
Paul S. Martin.

CONTENTS

To: Marcia Zubrow, my wife
    Anne and Reuben Zubrow, my parents

FOREWORD

One of the principal objectives of the Cummings Archaeology Series is to provide substantive case studies of important theoretical and methodological innovations. Although many programmatic statements and short articles have been published concerning the numerous exciting strides made by archaeologists in recent years, few full-length treatments of these new trends are available. Archaeologists can lecture to the point of exhaustion about revolutionary trends in the discipline, but without concrete examples, it is difficult for students to grasp the significance of new developments in archaeological thinking.

We believe that Ezra Zubrow's examination of prehistoric carrying capacity in the American Southwest will fill a major gap in the archaeological literature and will enable both professionals and students to see some of the best new trends in anthropological archaeology at work. Moreover, this is a time when scientific considerations of demography are reaching new levels of sophistication and general interest in population growth and "the limits to growth" are increasing rapidly. The appearance of a case study such as this which examines demographic changes over a lengthy period of time and relates them to environmental changes should be the cause of considerable excitement.

This study should be particularly useful in middle level courses in archaeological or anthropological theory and method, as well as in a wide variety of courses on New World prehistory. Other social science courses concerned with questions of demography and carrying capacity also could benefit by the use of this book.

Zubrow is eminently qualified to write this work. He is currently Assistant Professor of Anthropology at Stanford University. He received his Ph.D. from the University of Arizona in 1971 and has conducted archaeological fieldwork in both the Southwestern United States and Mexico. In addition, he is the author of several important publications, including *Population, Climate, and Contact in the New Mexican Pueblos* (1974), "Carrying Capacity and Dynamic Equilibrium in the Prehistoric Southwest" (1971), "Environment, Subsistence, and Society: The Changing Archaeological Perspective" (1972), and "Adequacy Criteria and Prediction in Archaeological Models" (1973).

We hope that Zubrow's study and others to follow in this series will serve as useful additions to the instructional literature which anthropological archaeologists and other scholars can employ in both undergraduate and graduate teaching. We are proud to have Ezra Zubrow's *Prehistoric Carrying Capacity* as one of our initial books because we believe that it is not a "mere" case study but an important contribution to the field of archaeology.

Cambridge, Massachusetts
June, 1974

JEREMY A. SABLOFF
C.C. LAMBERG-KARLOVSKY
Series Editors

PREFACE

The relationships between population and resources are critical to cultural development and competition. It does not matter whether cultures are prehistoric or modern, ethnographic isolates or complex civilizations; rural or urban, underdeveloped or developed. It is a universal that all cultures need resources to support their populations.

Throughout time human populations have been both energy consumers and producers. For the past, it is possible to trace the history of cultural development as the conquest and the expenditure of energy supplies and sources. For the future, it appears difficult to tell whether production will be able to meet the demands of the consumers. For the present, the term "energy crisis" is heard more and more frequently. Zero population growth, the ecology movement, and the oil crisis are just some of the aspects of the energy problem which have had recent national prominence. Thus, *Prehistoric Carrying Capacity*, which is a study of long-term population-resource relationships in an ecological framework, cannot help but have relevance to the present.

This study exemplifies aspects of an integrated approach to archaeology often termed the "new archaeology." The "new archaeology" originated as a deductive, formalist, and behavioristic approach to the study of the prehistoric past. It was an explicit attempt to change the discipline from a humanistic study to a social science. Historically, it began in the 1940s with W.W. Taylor's recognition of the inconsistency between many archaeologists' stated goals of explaining cultural processes and their actual conclusions which described archaeological data and placed it in appropriate regional chronologies. However, Taylor's beliefs were ignored for a decade. The "new archaeology" did not begin to gain acceptance until Lewis Binford actually operationalized, in a series of controversial studies, an integrated approach for developing and relating archaeological theory to actual data (Binford 1972).

This study of prehistoric carrying capacity begins in Chapter One with a brief theoretical history that provides a background to the variables and concepts necessary to understand the relationships between population and resources. Chapter Two develops the model of carrying capacity as a dynamic equilibrium system. Chapter Three states four hypotheses and explains their relationship to the model. Then the collection and presentation of data from Hay Hollow Valley is discussed in Chapter Four with consideration given to problems in methodology. Chapter Five incorporates the data to test the hypotheses. Chapter Six presents the simulation model and its results. Chapter Seven is a philosophical retrospective.

Case studies, such as this one, attempt to familiarize readers with topics of theoretical, methodological, and substantive interest by introducing examples of scientific research. By doing this I am attempting to tread that fine line between a formal research monograph and a textbook. Each of these forms, when well executed, make important contributions. However, when case studies fail, it is because they are written at the wrong level and thus they are a research monograph or a textbook in disguise. I assure the reader that *Prehistoric Carrying Capacity* is not a masked textbook and I hope it is not a research monograph in harlequin colors.

Few studies ever tell you how research actually originates. Research is a complex process dependent upon a whole series of factors including the researcher's personality, the social context in which he is working, the potential for funding, and the state of the discipline. Some of these factors, such as the interests of one's spouse or boredom, are totally extraneous to our ideal view of science or research.

The carrying capacity project began under the most inauspicious of circumstances. I was attending a seminar given by the late Professor Dozier and was listening half-heartedly to an exceptionally dull report by a fellow graduate student. I thought how strange—he is rambling on about kinship, moieties, clans, and lineages of the Southwestern Pueblos and he doesn't even know about how many people he is talking. I jotted down in my notes "what are the determinants of Pueblo population size" and fell back into a semi-conscious stupor until he finished his talk. Later, it was to become my major research interest and hopefully a contribution to the integrated research being attempted by various archaeologists at the University of Arizona.

For heuristic purposes, I believe that there are two basic approaches to research which at the risk of gross oversimplification, may be termed "isolationist" and integrationist." These approaches are characterized by different rationales, work habits, and problem determinants, each with its particular strengths and weaknesses. The isolationist is primarily in a dialogue with himself. The rationale for doing research is that it is interesting for the researcher and is necessary for his self-growth. He works alone in the field, in the laboratory or in his study. What determines his particular problem is his changing world view and interests. The strength of the isolationist approach is the opportunity for extended work into a set of related problems making possible a consistent, well-integrated solution. However, the weakness is that ideas become so privately elaborated that they are difficult to describe to others, and there is greater potential for lengthy explorations of nonproductive areas.

The integrationist is primarily in a dialogue with his colleagues and the discipline. The rationale for research is that a particular problem is theoretically or methodologically important. The problem is necessary to solve due to the state of the discipline or because it is of critical interest to a group of intellectual peers. The integrationist works in a small group or has other researchers with whom he may "bounce around" ideas. What determines the particular problem is a combination of group and individually held perceptions of a discipline and its productive future direction. This approach has the advantage of bringing more than one mind and a great multitude of talents to a single or group of related problems, thus reducing the probability of mistakes and enhancing communication. However, there is also a greater potential to be influenced by intellectual fads and valuable research time may evaporate into meaningless group meetings.

Significant research of international importance has been done using both strategies. "Isolationists" might include Marx, Pasteur, Curie, and Farraday. The impression one has of Marx sitting in the British Museum Reading Room, nursing his boils and carbuncles, and writing *Das Kapital* in isolation except for occasional visits from Engels is essentially correct. According to Sir Isiah Berlin (1939:104), one of Marx's most famous biographers; "After the debacle of 1848, he withdrew into an attitude of aggressive isolation, preserving contact only with men who had proved their personal loyalty to the cause with which he was identified." On the other hand, an example of the "integrationist" approach is the discovery of the structural model of DNA which made possible the biochemical solution to the genetic code. As Watson (1969:11) puts it, the solution was chiefly "a matter of five people: Maurice Wilkins, Rosalind Franklin, Linus Pauling, Francis Crick and me." These scientists not only shared an office but were in daily communication with other members of the Cavendish Laboratory of Cambridge University.

Arizona's Anthropology Department in the late 1960s provided an ideal situation for the development of an integrationist strategy. William Longacre, a student of Binford at Chicago, had come to Arizona after showing that it was possible to determine prehistoric social organization from material culture. Longacre's work was one of the best case studies of what has come to be called the "new archaeology." (See Binford 1972; Watson, Le Blanc, and Redman 1972; or Leone 1973.)

Longacre quickly gathered around him a small cadre of graduate students who felt it was their responsibility to show how productive this new paradigm developed by Binford and his students could be. The atmosphere at Arizona became electric because Longacre had come to do battle with the archaeological giants.

What was happening at Arizona was not unique. Similar centers were being developed at Santa Barbara by James Deetz, at UCLA by James Hill, at Michigan by Binford and Flannery, and was continuing with student leadership at Chicago. In addition, Paul Martin of the Field Museum and the Director of Southwestern Archaeological Expedition, one of the most prestigious members of the archaeological establishment, had decided to use his field research and field school as an experimental research and training ground for the "new archaeology." Thus, there was the continuing opportunity to design new research and to test new ideas and techniques in the field. These opportunities were expanded as numerous individuals began to get research grants and when Longacre took over the field school at Arizona.

What was critical at Arizona was that the intellectual organization determined the social organization. It was common to argue theory, methodology, and data not only in the classroom but in the halls or at parties. Similarly, there was an informal network that passed information between the various centers through friends, telephone messages, and an infinite number of letters. This made new techniques, problems, results, and failures known long before the published results. It was recognized early that this social organization should not determine intellectual organization. Too many intellectual movements have died because in the end there was only communication between friends and there was no new infusion of ideas. This was explicitly denied and active recruitment of new people with new ideas became part of the social organization.

It was in this context that this research began.

Stanford University
June, 1974

EZRA B. W. ZUBROW

ACKNOWLEDGMENTS

This study is based on work done at various times between 1967-1971. There are numerous people whose help and criticism should be recognized. I want to thank Dr. William A. Longacre, Dr. Jane H. Underwood, Dr. Raymond H. Thompson, Dr. Richard Hevly, and the late Dr. Edward P. Dozier for ideas, help and encouragement throughout the research and the many drafts of this study. I owe very special thanks to the late Dr. Paul S. Martin, Curator Emeritus of the Department of Anthropology of the Field Museum of Natural History, for the opportunity to work with the Southwest Archaeological Expedition and the use of the data derived therefrom. Of my many friends and colleagues from this expedition I wish to single out Dr. Mark Leone, Dr. Fred Plog, Dr. Craig Morris, and Daniel Bowman for special thanks. There are some eighty others who made significant contributions during this period. I am grateful to each. (See Zubrow 1971 for a complete listing.)

Since 1971 this study has benefited from the ideas and comments of Doctors A.J. Ammerman, Luca Cavalli-Sforza, George Collier, Charles Frake, and Bernard Siegel. The fine editorial hands of Dr. C.C. Lamberg-Karlovsky and Dr. Jeremy Sabloff have been an important contribution to the finished product, which it is a pleasure to acknowledge.

I am grateful to the following organizations which have generously provided monetary support, information, cooperation, and various types of data: the Field Museum of Natural History; National Defense Education Act-Title II; National Science Foundation and its Undergraduate Research Participation Program; United States Air Force Strategic Air Command; United States Bureau of Indian Affairs; United States Forest Service; United States Geological Survey; University of Arizona's Computer Center, Department of Anthropology, and Extension Division; and Stanford University.

1

A BRIEF THEORETICAL HISTORY

The relationship between resources and population has been a topic of research for the past 200 years. Optimists have emphasized that the increase in resources and output is the result of technological development, and they used examples from Western Europe after the industrial revolution. Pessimists, noting the underdeveloped areas of the world, cite countless examples where the standard of living and the income per capita have been steadily falling because the size of the population is surpassing economic production. The question is by no means moribund. As a perusal of the demographic and economic literature shows, it continues to be not only of scholarly interest (Duncan and Hauser 1959, Higgens 1968) but also of popular interest. Most recently, there has been a series of popular studies which suggest that the present exploitation of natural resources is close to the ultimate limits. The pessimism of these authors is reflected in their titles: *Famine 1975* (Paddock and Paddock 1967), *The Population Bomb* (Ehrlich 1969, and *Standing Room Only* (Sax 1955).

1

The study of the relationship between population and resources is complex, partially because there is a large number of variables which are difficult to differentiate. For example, the resources which a population has at its disposal are not simply a function of their presence in the environment. Members of a population must be conscious of the potential resources as a resource. There must also be a set of values and priorities which allow portions of or the entire population to decide to allocate its time, land, labor, and capital in exploitation of one particular resource rather than another. A population must have not only political and economic control but access to that part of the environment which contains the resource. It must also have sufficient technological sophistication for exploitation. There must be a social organization which is adequate to distribute the product which is obtained from the resource.

Not all of the above variables interact at the same time or place. Similarly, the growth of the population may not simply be a result of biological reproduction. The amount of growth may also be determined by disease, genetics, or density problems. In addition, growth has social and ideological components such as status hierarchies and birth control values. These factors may act singly or in any combination.

This complexity is reflected in the analyses which have been suggested to explain the relationship. The following brief history discusses the contributions of authors who have placed the primary explanatory emphasis of the population-resource problem on cultural, economic, and demographic variables, respectively.

ANTHROPOLOGICAL EXPLANATIONS

It is interesting to note that although there has been considerable theoretical analyses of the relationship between population and resources which use cultural variables, most of this work has not been done by anthropologists, but by economists. In fact, if one examines the literature of the major anthropological schools, it is difficult to discover references to the population resource question. One theoretical position in modern anthropological theory is that of the cultural evolutionists who state that competition deriving from population pressure is a major force in the evolution of social organization.[1] Generally, it is suggested that the increased complexity of social organization acts in a manner similar to an innovation to relieve the pressure of the law of diminishing returns.

Earlier anthropologists, however, saw different relationships and were by no means as unified in their positions. Spencer, in a short article entitled

---

[1] This has been espoused by Sumner and Keller (1927), Steward (1949), White (1959), Carnerio (1961) and, most recently, by Harner (1970).

"A Theory of Population" (1852), was a precursor of Marx in suggesting that man's intelligence would solve the overpopulation problem. He states intelligence is inversely related to fertility. Thus, as man moves through the stages of his evolutionary scheme towards perfection, intelligence increases and family size decreases.

Emile Durkheim (1933) believed that the competition derived from increasing population size and density was a threat to social solidarity. He took this concept from Darwin, who felt that competition was a result of number, density, and similarity between species, and applied it to society. Durkheim noted that large, highly dense populations that are organized into complex societies should not exist because the threat of competition between and among the parts of society would be too great. However, he recognizes that such complex societies do exist, and therefore, the competitive threat to social solidarity must have been averted. Durkheim believes that by increasing the division of labor, not only is production increased but more importantly one increases the heterogeneity of the society. Thus, the division of labor decreases the competition which is inherent in the otherwise increasing similarity between members of a growing society, and the social fabric is maintained.

Franz Boas, in the process of increasing anthropological empiricism, appears to take a self-contradictory stand. On one hand, he claims that his kinship studies resulted in "no evidence that density of population, stability of location, or economic status is necessarily connected with a particular system of relationship and of behavior connected with it." On the other hand, he recognized that polygyny played a distinct role in the expansion and cultural assimilation of the Arab population during the sixth and seventh centuries (Boas 1911).

Although diffusionists held a general interest in migration as a cultural transmitter, they did not examine its relationship to resources or its cultural determinants. Rather, they placed the primary emphasis upon the determination of when and where migrations took place and what cultural traits were transmitted. In fact, W.H. Rivers, a British diffusionist, attempted to explain the depopulation of Melanesia in an article entitled "The Psychological Factor" (1922). He believed that this depopulation, in spite of the existence of sufficient resources, was a result of a "loss of interest of life." Enforced contact without recourse destroyed native economic, social, and religious institutions, accompanied by a decreasing birth rate and an increasing death rate.

With the development of the culture area concept, Wissler (1917), and more importantly, Kroeber, attempted to empirically determine demographic characteristics of a specific culture area. Kroeber, in his classic, *Cultural and Natural Areas of Native North America* (1939), concluded that the existence of agriculture did not make significant differences in population density; indeed the coastal areas were much more densely populated than any other area of native North America.

The interest of the British structural-functionalists in the population re-source question was limited. Although Meyer Fortes in his "Demographic Field Study of the Ashanti" (1954), placed great emphasis upon population, his final explanation of Ashanti's high fertility rate relied upon the value sys-tem for deriving causal variables.

Ludwick Kryzwicki's *Primitive Society and Its Vital Statistics* (1934) is one of the most directly relevant publications in anthropological population resource literature and yet is not well-known in the United States. Kryzwicki, a professor of Social History at the University of Warsaw, devoted his intellec-tual talents to a demographic analysis of primitive communities and tribes. This work contains the most massive compilation of historical and ethnograph-ic population references of which the author is aware, summarized tribe by tribe in a 238-page appendix. Utilizing this mass of data, Kryzwicki was able to develop an evolutionary framework in which to analyze consequences of the relationship between social and demographic variables. He shows that so-cial factors, such as institutional differences, contribute to population isolation which in turn is responsible for the small size of the units of the tribal world. Simultaneously, the small size causes the high degree of social variability. Small changes in population composition force major changes in the social structure as clans and lineages die out. These factors mutually reinforce each other to keep primitive societies small and diverse. Kryzwicki is also a precur-sor of the "structural pose" concept in which he notes that tribal populations vary in size as the resources fluctuate seasonally.

Frank Lorimer is a demographer with a structural-functionalist approach to anthropological theory. He shows in *Culture and Human Fertility* (1954) that a prerequisite for successful expansion of pre-industrial societies is the ex-istence of the corporate unilineal kinship group which is directly related to high fertility. Lorimer notes that social and religious controls of fertility are dependent upon the marginality, the isolation, and limited subsistence base of a geographic area. His analysis of the function of social structure complements Wrigley. While E.A. Wrigley (1969) sees the function of social structure as a mechanism to distinguish surplus population, Lorimer discovers that societies with a well-developed formal social structure have higher fertility rates than those without. In fact, he finds that to the extent contact results in disorgani-zation of social structure, it also decreases fertility.

Joseph Birdsell has played a two-fold role in the development of the an-thropological insights into the population-resource question. In a study relat-ing environmental, cultural, and demographic variables to hunting and gather-ing, he shows that "for the simplest cultural levels, the densities of human pop-ulations are primarily determined by the variables of the environment" (Bird-sell 1953). In the Australian case, population density is determined by rainfall. On the basis of this and similar studies, he developed models to explain not only the growth, but the size and distribution of the Australian native popula-tions. Thus, he was among the first anthropologists to use formal models with predictive value and to test them using demographic variables over a considerable time depth. His second contribution is that as an educator he has inspired a series of students to carry out research on the population-resource question.

ECONOMIC AND RESOURCE ORIENTATION

In 1776, Adam Smith published *The Wealth of Nations* in which the market as a self-regulating equilibrium system was shown to result from two opposing forces. On one hand, self-interest acts to guide men into work for which society is prepared to pay. On the other, the regulating force is competition. A man whose self-interest is not checked is in financial trouble. If he overcharges for his wares, he has no buyers. If he underpays his workers, he has no employees. Furthermore, Smith suggested that the market mechanism tends to increase production, wealth, resources, and population partially because the market is a milieu which encourages innovations, inventions, expansions, and risks. But more importantly, this increase was the result of the law of accumulation and the law of population (Heilbroner 1961). The object of accumulation was reinvestment and thus growth, meaning more industry, machines, and a larger labor force. Given competition, accumulation resulted in a greater demand for labor and thus higher wages in turn producing lower profits and less accumulation. Smith solved this problem with the law of population which states labor, the bulk of population, is a commodity which follows the dictates of supply and demand. So as the labor force increases to the new demand or overshoots it, competition decreases wages, accumulation increases, and there is a new cycle of upward spiralling growth. Thus, there is to be expected a continual, but episodic growth of resources and population. This rise in the working class will force the population upwards, but not quite to, subsistence, as long as the accumulation process continues.

There was nothing in the population-resource relationship to shake the faith of the philosophers in the rationality of the future. Thomas Robert Malthus published in 1798 the famous *Essay on Population* and in one book not only changed the viewpoint of the age from rational optimism to pessimism, but inscribed his name with opprobrious connotations upon intellectual history (Heilbroner 1961). Taking the concept of equilibrium from Smith and applying it to population, he put forward the view that population when unchecked will increase geometrically due to the "inherent attraction between the sexes" (Boulding 1959). But sustenance increases only as an arithmetic ratio. Thus, the subsistence base eventually puts a limit upon the increasing population. Or, as Malthus himself succinctly stated:

> I think I may fairly make two postulata.
> First, that food is necessary to the existence of man.
> Second, that the passion between the sexes is necessary, and will remain nearly in its present state.

> Assuming, then, my postulata as granted, I say, that the
> power of population is indefinitely greater than the power
> in the earth to produce subsistence for man.

This limit is enforced through the "positive checks" of famine, disease, and war unless man utilizes what Malthus termed the "preventive checks," deferred marriage and celibacy. In other words, growth must end because there is increasing mortality or decreasing fertility. Malthus does not put too much faith in the latter, for he notes "Towards the extinction of the passion between the sexes, no progress whatever has hitherto been made." Thus, equilibrium is reached through increasing mortality and increasing mortality means increased misery and starvation. This gloomy prediction has come to be known as the "Dismal Theorem." Kenneth Boulding has stated it in other words, "if the only ultimate check on the growth of population is misery, then the population will grow until it is miserable enough to stop its growth" (Boulding 1959).

The gloom is never relieved for Malthus continues that any technical improvement such as a technological invention or an organizational change can only temporarily relieve misery. The relief from the subsistence situation will cause the population to grow until a new equilibrium at subsistence is reached. Thus, innovations and progress results simply in an increase in population enabling more people to live in misery than before. It is this corollary to the Malthusian doctrine which Boulding has labeled the "Utterly Dismal Theorem" (Boulding 1959).

Over the last hundred and fifty years, errors in the Malthusian theory have been pointed out. The arithmetic and geometric ratios were in error, but this is of little importance since the crucial principle is that resources must limit population. Whether this takes place in twenty-five years or two-hundred years is irrelevant except to those being limited. Historically, it is interesting to note that Malthus was aware of this inadequacy for he put far less emphasis on the ratios in his second edition of the *Essay* (Malthus 1803). More importantly, his hypothesis that each advance in technology is absorbed by a consequent increase in population, thus preventing any increase in the standard of living, was disproved by the industrial revolution. It is ironic that with the exception of nineteenth-century Ireland, the Malthusian spectre had been postponed in North America and Western Europe as he was writing his essay. In fact, the food supply has outrun the population growth as a result of a large increase in agricultural land and the remarkable rise of the yield of food per acre. Malthus had underestimated man's technological ingenuity and almost unlimited capacity to move himself and his goods. The Malthusian doctrine was, however, a valid empirical generalization for most of the world until the 1780s. But as a general law, it failed because of the fallacious assumption that increases in production could never exceed increases in population. Today its validity must be qualified by the concept of development. The applicability of the doctrine is inversely related to the degree of economic development a country has sustained. Before one simply rejects the utility of the Malthusian doctrine, one should examine the more recent formulations of this doctrine which will be considered in the demographic section of this chapter.

A friend of Malthus, David Ricardo, contributed the next major theoretical insight into the relationship between population and resources. Ricardo in the *Principles of Political Economy* (1911), agreed with the Malthusian doctrine on population growth, but asked what will be the distribution of wealth under Malthusian disequilibrium situations. Ricardo saw a tripartite of the economic world: (1) laborers labored and as recompense were paid wages, (2) capitalists organized and risked capital and in return received profits, and (3) the landlords received rents for the use of the soil. In fact, the landlord's income was not checked by competition. Rent was a return which had its origin in the fact that not all land was equally productive. Thus, two farms equal in all respects except soil may have different productivity. Since both farms sell the products in the same market, the difference in productivity expressed as market value will determine the rent value of the more productive farm. As population expands in the Malthusian disequilibrium situation, Ricardo suggests the margin of cultivation will move out to less productive lands. This theme will be developed in our study into the marginality hypothesis. As wages go up, the capitalist's profits go down. So Ricardo claims the result of the Malthusian disequilibrium is to benefit the landlords, hurt the capitalists, and leave the workers close to the subsistence margin.

The Marxian concept of the population-resource relationship is based upon the rejection of the Malthusian doctrine which Marx labeled a "libel on the human race." The proletariat, the future communists, were too intelligent to allow reproduction to decrease the standard of living. In addition, Marx's famous labor theory of value (1867) has implications for the relationship between population and resources. The premise is that production is at the basis of society. The labor theory of value states that the value of any commodity is dependent upon the labor involved in its production. Profit is the motivating force of the capitalist system and is defined in terms of labor. It is the difference between the value the laborer is paid for producing the commodity and the value he produces. Since the latter is the larger, Marx felt the laborer was short changed. Expansion of the system results in an increase of wages as the demand for labor rises. In order to maintain profits, labor saving machinery is introduced. But, its value is illusionary since actual profits are derived from the diminishing labor force. Labor, now underemployed, is willing to accept substandard wages. This is the origin of the business cycle which fluctuates in expanding booms and contracting depressions as the demand for labor increases and decreases. For Marx, it is the twin forces of technological change as represented by labor saving machinery and capital accumulation which enlarges the "reserve" army of the unemployed (Ranis 1963). By capital accumulation Marx means the accumulation of produced goods that may be used for further production. In short, for Marx, Malthusian population pressure is simply the result of capital accumulation, increasing less rapidly than the laboring population, i.e., the demand for labor is less than the size of the laboring class.

The neoclassical era in economic theory entailed a deemphasis upon the population-resource relationship as economic research was devoted to microtheory and equilibrium analysis (Duncan and Hauser 1959). Two contributions should be noted briefly which are relevant to later parts of our study. Alfred Marshall, in his *Principles of Economics* (1920), emphasized the importance of time as an essential element in the working out of the equilibrium process. One of the criteria which the data base of our study had to meet was sufficient time depth to allow homeostatic mechanisms to act. Marshall suggests that the usual state for an economy and thus for the relationship between population and resources is a state of balance, a state of nongrowth, an equilibrium condition. Schumpeter's *Theory of Economic Development* (1911) refined an old theme; a stimulus is necessary to cause a disequilibrium and is a prerequisite for growth. This stimulus is an innovation used for production and is the discontinuous "disturbance," which "forever alters and displaces the equilibrium state previously existing."

Maynard Keynes (1936) discovered the nonhomeostatic relationship of savings and investment. His work resulted in a reemphasis upon population growth and long-term technological change in "development theory." Harrod (1948) and Domar (1957), two of Keynes' students, developed a model for stable growth. In this model, the problem of stable development was sustaining a high rate of capital accumulation in the face of declining profits. Exogenous population growth functions in a reversed role to Malthusian doctrine. Population growth no longer inexorably keeps the standard of living down but functions as a mechanism to stimulate investment by new consumption needs, while Schumpeterian innovations act to frustrate diminishing returns.

DEMOGRAPHIC EXPLANATIONS

The neo-Malthusians (for example, Peacock and Boulding) have noted that it took an industrial revolution to disprove Malthus. Thus, in conservative agricultural or underdeveloped areas (such as the prehistoric and ethnohistoric Pueblos in the American Southwest) where the industrial revolution has not changed the potential for production by several quantum leaps, Malthusian doctrine may be still thought to apply. The concept of a stable standard of living at the subsistence level is rejected. However, the conclusion that population growth is a correlate of technological change is believed to be viable under pre-industrial conditions. If the economic forces are somewhat inevitable, as some members of the "dismal" science have suggested, a modern ecological model is appropriate. The Malthusian ratios are replaced by population pressures in a series of organized, spatially differentiated ecosystems, each with various levels of consumption expectations based upon food chains with internal and external ecological connections. This is still a "food pull" argument in the sense that the size of the food supply pulls the population up or down in order to meet the available subsistence supplies.

Boserup (1965) has reversed the neo-Malthusian "food pull" argument. Growth precedes and determines agricultural development, a "population push" explanation. The size of the population pushes the economic development, and subsistence needs are met. Boserup's argument is based upon the decreasing efficiency of labor (or more exactly, the application of the law of diminishing returns to labor). Her premises are, (1) steady population increase, (2) fixed land area, (3) a reservoir of agricultural techniques, (4) lower output per man hour following innovation in agriculture, and (5) a flexible division of time between leisure and work (Adams 1966). Given population increase, stress on production may be resolved through territorial expansion, technological advance and intensification. These decrease the amount of time that land is left fallow. Since expansion is limited, the food crises force the society to rely on the two latter factors. As noted in premise (4) above, technological innovation decreases output per man hour. Therefore, to increase food output there must be increased labor man-hours per capita and reduced leisure man-hours per capita. Population increase causes not only a decrease in the amount of time that land is left fallow but a change in labor scheduling. Increasing intensification is reflected in the form of land use ranging from the least intense "forest fallow," through "bush fallow," "short fallow," and "annual cropping," to the most intensive "multicropping." The long-term result is the support of the expanded population rather than increased efficiency or standard of living.

A third model developed out of attempts in the United States to test the Malthusian and neo-Malthusian doctrine empirically. The theory of growth cycles and transition combines "population pressure" with mathematical analysis. Raymond S. Pearl (1925) suggested that population grew not at a constant rate but with a variable rate. This viewpoint is similar to Toynbee's theories insofar as it uses the growth curve of biological organisms as a template. Pearl claimed:

> The long run tendency of population growth can be represented by a curve which starting from a previously established stationary level, representing the supporting capacity of its region at the prevailing level of culture, productive technique, and the standard of living—rises at first slowly, then at an increasing rate, finally leveling out as the curve approaches an upper asymptote which represents the supporting capacity of the environment at the last stage (requoted from Lorimer, 1963: 297).

The mathematical graph which describes this growth cycle is called the "logistic curve" and was suggested by P.F. Verhulst in 1845 (see Figure 1.1a). The crucial factor is spatial density and Pearl's experiments on fruit flies gave empirical validation to his theory.

Although never totally refuted in a critical attack, logistic theory was replaced by transition theory because of its inaccurate predictions towards the end of the elongated "s." The weakness was the assumption of initial station-

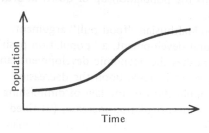

a. The result of Pearl's logistic growth cycle.

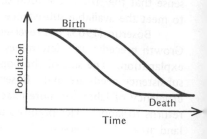

b. Probable cycle of births and deaths.

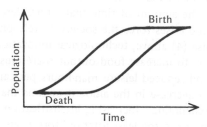

c. Improbable cycle of births and deaths.

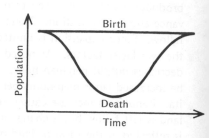

d. Malthusian cycle.

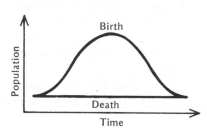

e. Baby boom cycle.

FIGURE 1.1   The logistic growth cycle.

ary growth rates and the empirical failure to locate examples of stable populations at the "upper asymptote." Harold Dorn (1950) tested the curve built from 1790-1940 and found the prediction for 1950 in significant error. F.K. Notestein (1945) noted that the gap caused by an initial decrease in deaths is closed and a new equilibrium is reached when a similar decline in fertility takes place. This transition between points of dynamic equilibrium explains the logistic curve for growth may be stimulated by an increased birth rate or a decreased death rate and terminated by either a decreased birth rate or an increased death rate (Cowgill 1949). (See Figures 1.1b and c.)

Although the theory fills the requirements of a high level analysis in that it is dynamic rather than static and it takes into account culture contact and social interaction, it has been criticized by Duncan and Hauser (1959:14):[2]

> As concerns explanation and especially prediction, however, transition theory ... has succeeded only in suggesting certain major complexes of poorly defined influences on components of population change ... The influences on population growth that it postulates are closely bound up with the particular historical circumstances of population growth in Western countries.

Analytical theory, although less well known outside of actuarial and demographic circles, has a history longer than that of the Malthusian theory. The theory developed in three major steps: (1) the development of life tables, (2) the recognition of the relation of a closed population with constant vital rates to its mortality schedule and rate of increase, and (3) the development of the systematic interrelationships between births, deaths, sex, and age structure. Halley, the astronomer, first produced the modern life table in the 1690s. These later became known as examples of "stationary populations," for the number of births equaled the number of deaths (Lorimer 1959).

In the 1760s, Euler, the Swiss mathematician, made the concept dynamic by showing that the age distribution could be determined by age-specific mortality and fertility rates whether the closed population was increasing, decreasing, or stationary. Finally, Lotka, in the twentieth century, developed a complete general theory of the interrelationships of the primary biological processes, including the determinants of age and sex structure, if one assumed constant age-sex specific mortality rates and fertility rates and a constant sex ratio at birth (1925, 1939).

Lewis Johnston attempted to apply Lotka's models to Navajo population with ethnographic and ethnohistoric data. He explains the failure of these models as follows:

> In the first place, the basic mortality rates from which the several United Nations model life tables were developed are heavily weighted by age-specific mortality levels reported among European countries since 1920. One can certainly question the degree to which these largely European rates would pertain to the members of a population such as the Navajo, whose entire mode and condition of life are so different. Second, the selection of the most appropriate model or group of models to represent a specific population at a particular time in its development is confronted with great difficulties when we lack reliable information on precisely those values which we need in guiding our selection ... (that is) ... fairly precise knowledge of the infant or early childhood mortality (Johnston, 1966:180).

---

[2] A similar criticism is applicable to "Gini's parabolic curve," an alternate but similar theory to the logistic curve (1930).

TABLE 1.1   Summary of theoretical contributions.

ANTHROPOLOGY	ECONOMICS	DEMOGRAPHY
White, Steward et al: Population pressure as a determinant of social organization which relieves diminishing returns.	*Smith:* Equilibrium.	*Neo-Malthusian:* The historical and underdeveloped area validity and the ecological ramifications of Malthusian doctrine.
Spencer: Intelligence is inversely related to fertility.	*Malthus:* Resources as a limiting factor.	*Boserup:* Population growth precedes and determines technological development and labor intensification.
Durkheim: The division of labor as a density and competition relief measure.	*Ricardo:* Distribution of resource for Malthusian disequilibrium.	*Pearl:* The lower logistic curve and the density dependence of growth.
Boas: Population density is not related to kinship.	*Marx:* Exogenous population growth.	*Dorn:* Testing the logistic curve.
Rivers: "Loss of interest" casued depopulation; value systems responsible for fertility rates.	*Marshall:* Time depth of equilibrium.	*Notestein:* Transition theory.
Kroeber: The agriculture density noncorrelation.	*Schumpeter:* Innovations as a stimulus for disequilibrium.	*Cowgill:* Logistic growth cycles.
Fortes: Value systems responsible for fertility rates.	*Keynes:* Nonhomeostatic relationship of savings and investment and reemphasis upon population growth.	*Lotka:* Stationary population models.
Kryzwicki: The isolation, size, social variability, reinforcement mechanism.	*Harrod:* Exogenous population.	
Lorimer: The expansion-unilateral kinship group, fertility relationship, the marginality controlled fertility relationship, the social organization fertility relationship.	*Domar:* Growth as a Malthusian reversal.	
Birdsell: Model building.		

This chapter has attempted to examine the major cultural, economic, and demographic concepts of the relationships between population and resources.[3] (See Table 1.1 for a capsule summary of most of the major ideas.) Clearly, the problem is a complex one. Any model which will purport to explain such interrelationships must be general enough to incorporate many of the ideas presented in this chapter. However, in order that the analyst is not left in a welter of conflicting theory, the model must be sufficiently specific and operational as to be testable. The concepts and variables do not always relate to each other nor do they always interact at the same time or place. Thus, the model must also be designed to use any or all of these concepts and the variables for a particular test. This model is developed in the following chapter.

----

[3] The most complete theoretical summary extant is the United Nations publication, *The Determinants and Consequence of Population Trends: A Summary of the Findings of Studies on the Relationships Between Population Changes and Economic and Social Conditions*, 1955, in which the work of over 1500 authors is summarized. In separate chapters, it differentiates the economic and social causes and concomitants of growth, fertility, mortality, age structure, distribution, labor consumption, and output.

2

THE MODEL

THEORETICAL DEFINITIONS AND ASSUMPTIONS

The concept of carrying capacity is complex.[1] **Carrying capacity is the maximum size of a population which can be maintained indefinitely within an area.** Since there is a tendency toward the maintenance of a state of balance, carrying capacity may be measured in terms of equilibrium. This balance is a consequence of opposite forces counteracting each other, resulting in a diminishing net change or a stable constant. It is dynamic in that the state of balance may take on different values and change over time and space. Therefore, **carrying capacity is a dynamic equilibrium system.**[2]

---

[1] The non-specialist conceives of carrying capacity as the maximum amount of organisms or biomass that the land can support. This is an aggregate viewpoint because it combines species. It is not accurate because the term is population specific.

[2] This viewpoint is not universally accepted. For those interested in the debate the reader is referred to the original position papers both pro (L.B. Slobodkin, F.E. Smith and N.G. Hairston 1967) and con (W.W. Murdock 1960; P.R. Ehrlich and L.C. Birch 1967).   15

Before one may discuss a model of carrying capacity as a dynamic equilibrium system, it is necessary to delineate some of the basic assumptions and definitions under which the model will be built. The assumption-base is partly a consequence of the **definition of a model**, partly of the **type of model**, partly of the **data base** on which the model is to be tested.

Definition of a Model

Starting with the most general, a model is defined as a simulation of reality that is simplified to facilitate the understanding of complex processes. More accurately, **theoretical models are sets of hypotheses which simplify complex observations by offering a largely predictive framework which structures the observations to isolate the important information from the irrelevant** (Clarke 1968). This isolation process is partially accomplished by ignoring observations outside of the defined universe of study.

The first assumption, then, in building the model is that one may define a specific universe through a set of criteria which divide the entire universe of potential data into relevant subsets. The universe which is used in this study is the Hay Hollow Valley in east-central Arizona between A.D. 0-1450. A specific segment of cultural history has been delineated by using geographic and temporal partitioning criteria. The second assumption is that it is possible to define a set of variables which are general enough to allow the deductive generation of hypotheses, but specific enough for an adequate description of the system.

Type of Model

In this study a **systems model** will be used. Systems models are particularly applicable to such problems as the population-resource relationship for several reasons. First, *General Systems Theory* is a level of theoretical model building that lies between the highly generalized construction of pure mathematics and specific theories of specialized disciplines (Boulding 1968). It is true that the greater the generality, the less the content. But, the specializations of fields and subfields in many disciplines do not reach sufficient generality to allow advances in other disciplines to have any effect on them because there is no connecting bridge. Systems theory acts as a connecting bridge. Numerous theories in many disciplines have made contributions to the resource-population question. Thus, the comprehensive model in this study, acting as a bridge, will attempt to use some of the specific contributions of the theoretical history previously discussed (see Table 1.1).

Second, General Systems Theory has been derived both deductively (Ashby 1968) and inductively (Bertalanffy 1968). Historically, it was generated to answer a set of problems in the nonphysical and behavioral sciences. It was realized that with the exception of evolution, the lack of laws was only partially a result of the complexity of the variation in nonphysical data. Although there is order to the data, the order itself varies in its organization, maintenance, and changes. This problem is augmented since causality at the nonphysical level is not necessarily a one-way affair. In other words, if one may state that social phenomenon A causes B, it does not preclude that social phenomenon B may also cause A.

These problems were answered with the development of cybernetics, the study of homeostatic mechanisms; information theory, which allows information to be quantified as negative entropy; and game and decision theory, which allows competition and choices to be expressed in quantified form. These approaches made possible the analysis and quantification of types of behavior which had been impossible to examine before. Inductively, sophisticated "data crunching" techniques, such as factor analyses and a variety of discriminant analyses, have made possible the isolation of both principle and minor components of multivariate phenomena. Thus, not only complex behavior but complex data become potentially understandable in more simplified terms. In short, General Systems Theory allows one to operationalize concepts which are applicable to organized wholes including interaction, centralization, competition, and finality from a general definition of systems as a complex of interacting components.

Third, General Systems Theory allows one to transcend the boundary between living and physical sciences by having a similar theory for open and closed systems. Closed systems are defined as open systems with a zero value for input. Systems may be defined informally or formally. At the most informal level it will suffice to state that systems are a set of components and relationships, inputs and outputs. Hall and Fagan (1968) and Wymore (1967) have defined a system more formally. **A system is a set of objects and their relationships between the objects and between their attributes.** Objects are part of the system. Attributes are defined as the properties of objects. The environment is the set of all objects which change the system or are changed by it.

Hall and Fagan classify systems into the following categories: "Adaptive systems" are open systems which are not teleological but pseudo-teleological. "Compatible systems" are defined as those systems which reflect the best adaptation to environment. Any system with a stochastic variable constitutes a "system with randomness." Finally, "isomorphic systems" are those systems in which there is a one to one relationship between components and relationships. **The model used in this study is an open, compatible, optimization system with stochastic variables.**

The Data Base

The **data base** upon which the model will be tested is part of a pre-Columbian cultural tradition located in the American Southwest. Rather than attempt a definition of culture since there are almost as many definitions as anthropologists (Kroeber and Kluckhohn 1952), the focus will be upon the broad behavioristic categories which are directly relevant to the model.

Modifying Otis Duncan's (1959) simplified model of human ecology, there are four mutually articulated categories: resources, organization, technology, and population. **Resources are defined as the aggregate of all nonhuman external conditions which influence or modify the existence of the human population under consideration.** Thus, it may include nonliving phenomena such as topography, climate, and hydrology; botanical phenomena such as trees and grasses, and zoological phenomena of all sizes. Resources are differentiated from the environment. The term environment is being withheld for use in its specific systemic sense. At times the two, resources and environment, may be isomorphic, that is, similar in form but different in function or in origin. However, resources will be considered as components within the system, while environment is outside of the system.

Organization is defined as all the cultural phenomena which allow a human population to maintain its corporate nontechnological identity. These include social structure, language, and religion. More generally, it is possible to define organization in systemic terms. The theory of organization is partly coextensive with the theory of functions of more than one variable (Ashby 1968). Organization exists: (1) when the relation of the variables A to B is dependent upon C's value or state, or (2) when there is some constraint in the product space of the variable possibilities. When organization exists (for example, a function) there are no longer two independent variables and the product space is limited. The two ends of the continuum are, respectively, organized simplicity, or chaotic complexity (Rappaport and Hovarth 1968:73). Entropy is a measure of homogeneity. Thus, organization may be measured as negative entropy. Organization thus implies a decrease in potential diversity. This, of course, is the opposite of the anthropological structural-functionalist viewpoint which maintains that organization is something extra, something added to the basic units or variables.

The reason technology is considered as a separate category rather than subordinating it as a subsystem of organization is not to imply its greater importance as compared to the other subsystems. Rather, the justification is that one of the major connections between the environment and the population is through the subsistence base whose production is a function of technology. Thus, **an operational definition of technology would be the systematic knowledge and culturally shaped material artifacts which allow humans to cope with their environment and each other in both constructive and destructive ways.**

Following Claude Villee (1962) who defines a population as a group of organisms of the same species which occupy a given area, that is, a residential population, **one may define a human population ecologically as the members of *Homo sapiens* within the area bounded by a biotic community.** Human populations, in common with all biological populations, have characteristics which are the function of the group as a whole and not of the individuals which compose the group. These are growth and dispersion rates, birth and death rates, population size and density, biotic potential, and age distribution.

One of the advantages of isolating population variables is that the population concept is not only modern (Simpson 1957), but has wide ramifications and applications throughout many branches of science (Boulding 1950). It is easier to relate the theory of several disciplines in an interdisciplinary approach when, as already mentioned, a bridge or common unit exists. First, within some of the natural sciences (ecology, zoology, and physical anthropology), and social sciences (demography, cultural anthropology, and economics) there is the generic concept "population." It is the common focus for anyone viewing a universe of phenomena comprising recognizable individual elements but concerned with such group attributes as number, composition, distribution, and change. Second, the population as a unit is highly amenable to quantitative analysis, since in the most abstract sense the concept was developed in statistical "renewal" and "sampling" theory. Renewal theory refers to deterministic and stochastic models of generalized accretion and depletion. Sampling theory was developed to meet the need for a criteria of representativeness where rigorous inferences about the composition and dynamics of a population may be based upon observations of a small percentage of the population.

The final assumption derived from the cultural data base is that it is possible to estimate prehistoric populations and resources through indirect indices. Archaeological surveys have traditionally served two functions. First, they provide the archaeologist with an approximation of the unexcavated material remains. These surveys may be limited in scope to a single site or they may embrace a wide variety of settlements or activity areas in a region. They are a crude method, perhaps, of measuring absolute population size; but, less crude for relative population size. The more intensively an area is surveyed and the more systematically it is sampled, the more refined is the estimate. There are a variety of effective indirect indices for monitoring the changes in prehistoric resource systems. They include such diverse techniques as dendroclimatology, palynology, vertebrate anatomy, and faunal analysis, as well as a variety of biochemical analyses. This study places considerable emphasis on pollen analysis.

The theory below and its models were developed in the following manner. First, there was an attempt to examine what would be the processes underlying the theory of carrying capacity as a dynamic equilibrium system by the use of graphs. Second, after this complete graphical analysis was developed, there was an attempt to restate the processes in terms of their mathematical equations. Third, these equations were modeled into actual systems that could be simulated. For each of these stages, we began with a highly simplified case, an ideal case, and then we added complexities which usually took the form of new processes or variables.

The following material is organized so as to give a step-by-step understanding of the development of the theory. First, a **simplified theory** is discussed and its model **(Version 1)** is presented. (Some of the mathematical equations are presented in Appendix I.) Then, the concepts and variables are added to build an **expanded theory,** which is also presented in a model **(Version 2).** This process of adding new concepts and variables is repeated for the next level, the **elaborated theory** and its model **(Version 3).** We expand the theory for the final time into the **comprehensive theory** and its model **(Version 4).**

THE SIMPLIFIED THEORY

Population—Resources

At the beginning of this chapter carrying capacity was defined as the maximum population that a region could support indefinitely—a balance between resource and population, a dynamic equilibrium system. What are the two opposing forces which determine the equilibrium? On one hand, the "prime dynamic mover" appears to be reproduction. This ability of all population to grow is called the biotic potential. On the other hand, Liebig's extended law states population is determined by the maxima and minima of specific resources (Boughey 1968:2). When some factor of the environment becomes limiting and the birth rate decreases (or the mortality rate increases, or both), then there is a regulatory influence of environmental resistance on the biotic potential. **Theoretically, a population will tend to keep reproducing until an ultimate limit is reached which is determined by the available supply of nutrients and energy.** Thus, the biotic potential is checked under natural and even under cultural circumstances. When there is a change in the supply of nutrients and energy, a change in the carrying capacity results, and there is a consequent growth or decrease of the biomass until a new equilibrium is reached.

Let us begin with a highly simplified case and gradually add complexities. There is a single population of human beings subsisting within a circumscribed area. This population is growing through time. The area is homogeneous and on it grows only a single species of plant (a resource) which the population consumes. Each year the area supports the same number of plants. The consumption of the resource is proportional to the population growth. The population size and the resources can be measured in the same unit, such as calories (a measure of energy). For example, a person needs approximately 2400 kilocalories a day to survive, while a square meter of a very productive corn field may produce a kilogram of corn, that is, 3630 kilocalories of edible food per year. Obviously, a larger population of say 100 adults needs a much larger supply of food for a year—in this case, 87,600,000 kilocalories or 24,132 kilograms of corn. Figure 2.1 shows this relationship between a resource which is constant over time and population growth. A denotes the carrying capacity point. The population grows until it reaches the carrying capacity point A, at time 5, and then it continues at the same level.

There is no *a priori* reason to assume that the resource needs to be at the particular level shown in Figure 2.1. For example, if there is an increase in the resource level soon after carrying capacity was reached, one would expect a disequilibrium situation in which the resources level was greater than the population. One would expect the population to grow along the population curve until a new equilibrium point *B* is reached (Figure 2.2). It is clear that the relationships could be changed so that the higher resource level occurs first and the population must decrease to reach the new lower resource level (Figure 2.3). Similarly, one may predict what would happen in other cases such as a change in the population curve. An increase (carrying capacity point *C*) or decrease (carrying capacity point *D*) in the population growth rate, which could be a consequence of a high status given to children or birth control, respectively, changes the shape of the curve and effects the time to carrying capacity, as in Figure 2.4. It is possible for the population to exceed the resource base for short periods of time. However, the four horsemen of the Apocalypse—death, war, famine, and plague—will reduce the population, as in Figure 2.5.

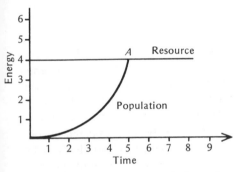

FIGURE 2.1   A simplified model of carrying capacity showing the relationship between population size and a resource which is constant through time. *A* = carrying capacity point.

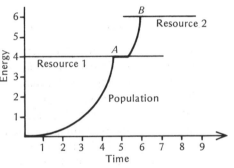

FIGURE 2.2   A simplified model of carrying capacity showing the relationship between population size and an increased resource base through time. *A* and *B* = carrying capacity points.

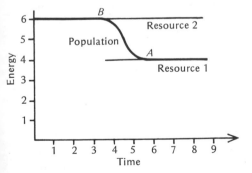

FIGURE 2.3   A simplified model of carrying capacity showing the relationship between population size and a decreased resource base through time. *A* and *B* = carrying capacity points.

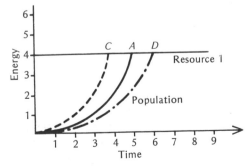

FIGURE 2.4   A simplified model of carrying capacity showing the effect of changing population growth rates. *A*, *C*, and *D* = carrying capacity points.

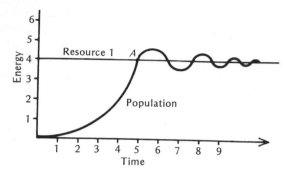

FIGURE 2.5   A simplified model of carrying capacity showing the population growing, exceeding the carrying capacity *(A)*, and then adjusting homeostatically to the carrying capacity.

Systemic Model—Version 1

An alternative representation of the same model is presented in the flow chart of Figure 2.6. Several points are worth noting. First, here the model is simplified and many steps are omitted. For example, if a population is greater than the resources, the negative growth rate may be a result of a decreased birth rate, an increased mortality rate, or an increased out-migration rate. Neither the growth rate algorithm, nor the migration factor is being considered in this flow chart. Similarly, the term "resource" glosses over several problems such as the reality of a multiple resource environment, what percentage of the resource base is usable, and what percentage of the usable resource base is perceived as usable. Second, the placement of the additional function (population = population + growth) before rather than after the decision node, builds into the model the possibility of greater homeostatic fluctuation. This is justified in that the growth rate is an *a posteriori* rather than *a priori* function. Populations do not usually decrease their growth rate because "they think" that the growth will result in insufficient resources, but because the growth rate has resulted in insufficient resources.

ADDITIONAL VARIABLES—SIMPLIFIED THEORY

Constant and Available Resources

Resources are a complex problem even in a simplified model. In the previous discussion, the portrayal of the resource has been as an inexhaustible but constant quantity. This is similar to the old problem of what happens when you subtract all of the odd numbers from an infinite set of all numbers. You still have an infinite set of numbers. The consumption of energy by the population has made no difference in the amount of energy that represents the resource.

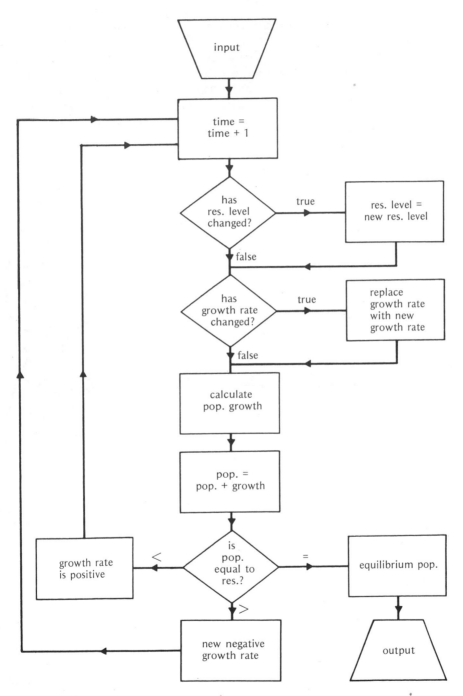

FIGURE 2.6   The simplified model of carrying capacity as a dynamic equilibrium system—
Systemic Model: Version 1. (pop. = population; res. = resource)

However, the reality is that consumption does deplete resources. Thus, let us examine the opposite extreme, namely that the resource is nonrenewable. We see that the critical variable is not the initial resource level but **the available resources which is the amount left over after consumption for future consumption by the population. This value limits the population size and thus is the effective regulator of carrying capacity.** Figure 2.7 shows the relationship between population growth, available resources, and the carrying capacity point. One should note that if the resource is nonrenewable, the carrying capacity is greatly reduced. As in the model with inexhaustible resources, it is possible for the resource curves and population curves to change (Figure 2.8). In addition, the same homeostatic processes exist which tend to force the population toward the carrying capacity point. However, these processes act faster in the nonrenewable case.

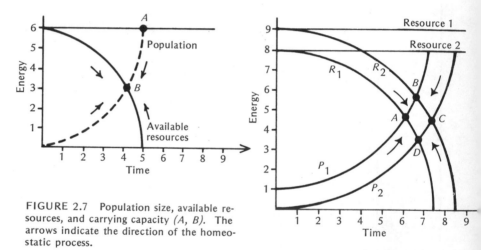

FIGURE 2.7   Population size, available resources, and carrying capacity *(A, B)*. The arrows indicate the direction of the homeostatic process.

FIGURE 2.8   Changing population *(P)*, growth rates, available resources *(R)*, and carrying capacities *(A, B, C, D)*.

Production

The production function is a technical economic law relating output to input. Given certain amounts of inputs such as labor, land, and capital, there are various amounts of a particular good or output which can be obtained. The amount varies with the level of technology. At any one level of technology, there will always be a maximum obtainable amount of product for any given amount of input, or conversely, there are a minimum set of inputs which will result in a particular output (Samuelson 1961).

The model which will be developed in this study considers production to be primarily a function of labor and land. It puts minimum emphasis on capital. This emphasis is based upon the well-documented lack of capital elasticity in underdeveloped peasant subsistence populations (Wolf 1966; Heilbroner 1962; Rostow 1962; Bauer and Yamey 1957; United Nations 1953). After defining the relationship between population and labor, it is possible to redefine the relationship between resources and population in terms of "isoproduction" curves (Figure 2.9). Every point on the curve equals the same amount of production.

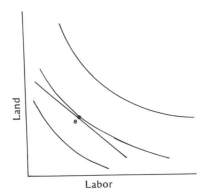

FIGURE 2.9   The smallest land-labor combination which will produce a particular output, at point *e*.

It is important to realize that the growth of production is not potentially infinite if one of the multiple inputs is fixed. The **law of diminishing returns** states that:

> An increase in some inputs relative to fixed inputs will cause total output to increase; but after a point the extra output resulting from the same additions of extra inputs is likely to become less and less. This falling off of extra returns is a consequence of the fact that the new "doses" of varying resources have less and less of the fixed resources to work with (Samuelson 1961:26).

This law has two major implications for our model. First, if one may assume that at least one factor input is fixed, then an increasingly labor intensive solution to a Malthusian disequilibrium caused by a population surplus is just a postponement and not a solution at all. Second, it will tend to reduce the amount of homeostatic fluctuation around the model's equilibrium points. An addition in population not only consumes more resources, but, if it is past the point of diminishing returns, it does not result in an equivalent addition to production as would an equal increase of population below the point of diminishing returns.

In contrast to the dampening effect of the law of diminishing returns, it is necessary to juxtapose the *increasing savings of scale*. This refers to a special type of increased production that results when all the factor inputs are increased. Savings of scale are the result of the economies of mass production and involve the savings derived from increased specialization, the use of interchangeable parts, and the breakdown of complex processes into repetitive simple operations (Samuelson 1961:26). It is special because the increase of output production is greater than the increase in factor input. Savings of scale are the rationale for the importance of Ford's conveyor lines and his "cheap car." However, in the model the role of "savings of scale" will be less important than the "law of diminishing returns." There are few operations of subsistence in either hunting and gathering, or peasant economies which are amenable to this type of production.

The Connection to Malthus and Neo-Malthusian Theory

As previously pointed out, the primary weakness of the original Malthusian doctrine was its application to a universal data base. In postindustrial economies increased savings of scale and technical innovations raised the level of production to such heights that the Malthusian checks were virtually bypassed. However, in the preindustrial societies where a much greater percentage of production is devoted to subsistence and where the margin of economic error must be smaller, the reality of the Malthusian spectre has never been seriously challenged. The actual existence of Malthusian disequilibria have been documented both historically (the Irish potato famine), and ethnographically (the critical underdevelopment in India).

As our ecological model is expanded, it will become apparent that it is not simply a restatement of the Malthusian model, but it is an extension. The concept of ecological equilibrium is derived from the Malthusian system. Similarly, Darwinian evolution may be perceived as ecological succession. Small chance and adaptive biological or cultural variations produce constant and irreversible changes in the equilibrium values of the populations of all species or cultures (Boulding 1959). Thus the equilibrium concept is also generalized and is able to generate evolutionary results.

Neo-Malthusian models have both advantages and disadvantages. The primary advantages are that given the initial conditions one may predict the expected consequences and one may quantify both the initial conditions and the expected results. The primary disadvantage of this type of neo-Malthusian model building is that contemporary demographic and ecological data do not lend themselves to testing the model. This is because the time span for which the data exists scarcely suffices to encompass long-term ecological processes. In addition, modern technological development with its concomitant diversity of resources, complex trade patterns, and ease of mobility complicate the data to the point that it is necessary to utilize factor and discriminant analyses to remove the masking data patterns and variables.

Archaeology and ethnohistory are thus in a unique position to evaluate this type of model. Their data span long time periods and some of the societies they consider have not developed the complex resource networks, trade systems, and technologies which distinguish our modern industrial nation states.

EXPANDED THEORY

Spatial Variation—Homogeneous and Heterogeneous Resource Bases

As presented initially the model is over-simplified. It may be viewed as the relationship between two functions, a population function and a resource function. Since both functions change through time, their mutual solution, or graphically, the point of intersection, may also change through time, thus tracing out a series of equilibria. It does not take into account many variables such as spatial differentiation in resource patterns or multiple resource bases. First, one should examine the implications of the spatial differentiation of resources holding the temporal changes in the resource base constant. One may imagine a complex heterogeneous available resource pattern as exemplified by Figure 2.10 where there are four distinct resources separated spatially. If this complex pattern is divided into a set of homogeneous resource spaces (which we will call resource zones), it will be easier to build the more generalized model. The simplified model presented in Figures 2.1-2.5 accounts for only one resource zone. In order to account for the heterogeneous pattern, it is necessary to sum the models of the individual resource zones. This is exemplified in Figure 2.10 **where the total carrying capacity for the heterogeneous area is the sum of the individual resource zone carrying capacities.** This can be stated as $E = A + B + C + D.$

Multiple resources within a single zone do not need to be spatially differentiated. However, the additive principle noted above applies as well to this case. See Figure 2.11.

Temporal Variation

When the temporal variable is added, external conditions, such as climate, may cause different available resource curves to exist at different points in the chronology. Thus, over time there might be changes in the individual resource zone curves. Simultaneously, changes in fertility rates, abortion rate, or other demographic variables may result in changes in the population curves over time. Either resource or population curve changes will result in changes in the summation curves. These changes which may not be uniform are caused by exogenous factors that may be qualitatively different from the normal changes predictable by the functions.

Migration and Population Development at the Zonal Level

It has often been noted that through time the distribution of settlements follows a definite pattern that is partially dependent upon the spatial distribution

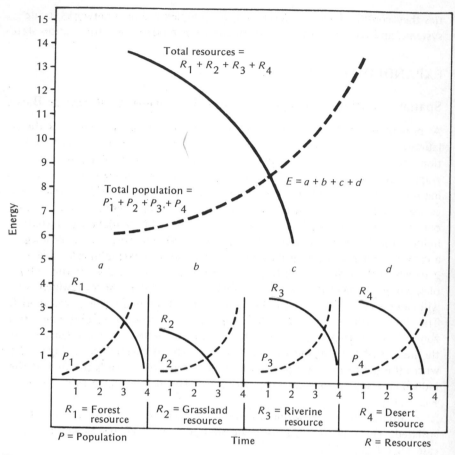

FIGURE 2.10 Heterogeneous resource model with four available resources which are temporally simultaneous but spatially separated into four resource zones. The model also shows the regional total.

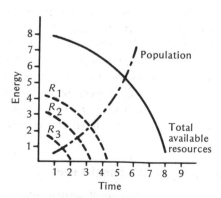

FIGURE 2.11 Multiple available resources, R_1, R_2, R_3, total available resources, and population size within a resource zone.

of resources (Kroeber 1939; Hagget 1966). One hypothesis to be examined is that **the development of populations in marginal resource zones is a function of optimal zone exploitation.**

In order to operationalize this hypothesis in terms of the model, one must set up a series of resource zones with consecutively diminishing total available resource curves as in Figure 2.12. It is easy to define at this point what is meant by optimal and marginal resource zones within the model's framework. **The optimal resource zone is the zone with the highest resource curve.** All other zones are marginal; the lower the resource curve, the more marginal the resource zone.

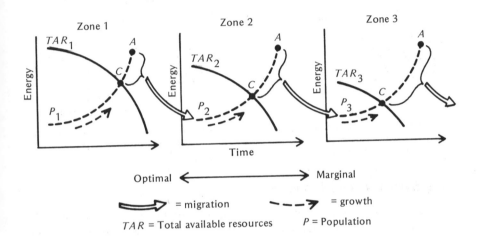

FIGURE 2.12   Predicted migration pattern.

One may predict on the basis of the model what will happen as a population starts to grow in the optimal resource zone (Figure 2.12). If the population is less than the carrying capacity, it will increase until it reaches the carrying capacity. If the population overshoots the carrying capacity as a result of population growth combined with immigration, then the population surplus (the distance C to A in Figure 2.12) has two alternatives: gradual extinction or out-migration to the next zone which is more marginal. In the more marginal zone the process would repeat itself. But each time there is movement from a zone to a more marginal zone, less population is necessary to reach carrying capacity. If there is no change in the resource curves over time one would expect the following sequence of events: first, a population fills up the optimal zone to carrying capacity; then a little later a second zone fills up to a smaller carrying capacity, and then a little later a third zone fills up. This process continues until all the zones are filled. There are indications, however, discussed by Birdsell (1957), Stott (1969), and Isard (1960), that the out-migration process might begin shortly before carrying capacity is reached because population pressure would have begun. On the basis of the model, the predicted population curves by zone would be similar to Figure 2.13. Note how similar these curves are to the logistic curve (Figure 1.1).

However, one must remember that the resource curves have been held constant through time. If they should begin to drop, the resulting carrying capacity decrease would result in a larger out-migration. This possibility is diagrammed in Figure 2.14.

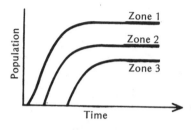

FIGURE 2.13   Predicted population curves by microhabitat or ecological zone with constant resources.

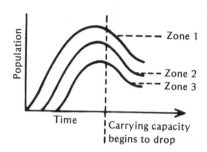

FIGURE 2.14   Predicted population curves by microhabitat or ecological zone with diminishing resources.

The Systemic Model—Version 2

Figure 2.15 presents the second version of the systemic model which includes the addition of spatial variation, temporal variation, and migration and population development at the zonal level.

THE ELABORATED THEORY

Economic and Demographic Variables

When relating demographic and cultural variables, the situation becomes more complex. Joseph Spengler in *Economics and Demography* (1959) has attempted to integrate the two disciplines by listing economic and demographic variables and showing their broad convergence. The demographic variables are differentially sensitive to changes in the economic variables. Emigration, immigration, internal migration, and differential internal migration, respectively, are the most sensitive for the decision process of the household since these variables are directly based upon the perceived economic situation and the potential of the area. Mortality, fertility, and total population are less directly determined.

Underlying Spengler's analysis are two basic economic definitions which are based upon the circular flow of economic goods and services within a society. First, net national product may be defined as the summation of consump-

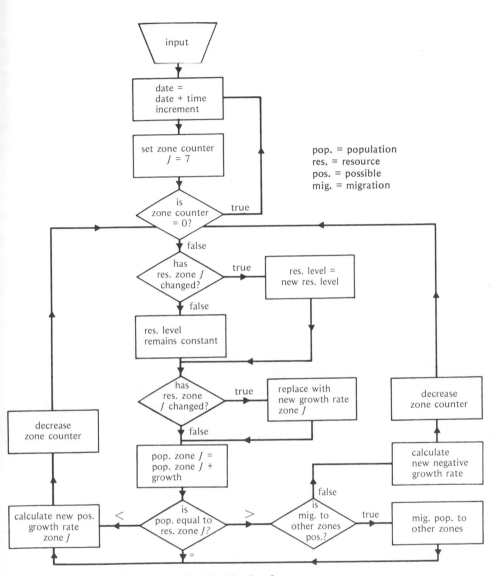

FIGURE 2.15   The Systemic Model: Version 2.

tion, investment, and governmental expenditure, or, second, it may be defined as the summation of the factors of production—wages, interest, profits, and rents (Samuelson 1961).

For the purposes of the model, it is easier to use the consumption rather than the earnings or income approach. It is necessary to redefine these variables in order to make them applicable to nonmonetary societies. Consumption causes no insurmountable problems since it may be calculated using biological necessities. Consumption of manufactured products such as Cheerios or household furnishings for industrialized societies is not different in form than the consump tion of food and firewood for peasant societies. The analogy does not hold equally well for income or the returns for labor, and it is far more difficult to estimate. Economists define investment as the outlaying of resources and the deferring of present consumption in order to obtain a gain in net real capital. For our model, the definition needs to be amended by replacing the word capital with resources. The definition then reads, for preindustrial societies, "investment" is the deferred use of resources, resulting in a net gain in usable resources which is greater than the gain that would have been derived from their immediate use. The storage of agricultural seed is an example. Finally, the concept of governmental expenditure must be redefined to organizational expenditure which allows for the variety of religious and social guises that governmental forms take in nonmonetary economies. Thus, the new formula is the net societal product is equal to consumption plus investment plus organizational expenditure.

Environment is defined as a systemic external variable in the original set of definitions. Resources are defined as the potential or real aggregate of all nonhuman external conditions which influence or modify the existence of the human population under consideration. Those resources which are actually used are part of the net societal product which in turn may be less than or equal to but never greater than available resources. The curves in Figures 2.1-2.11 should now be redefined in terms of the net societal product (NSP) whose relationship to available resources in the model is shown in Figure 2.16. The total net societal product for a resource zone is divisible into its component factors which are analogous to the total available resources of a resource zone. It also varies over time and space in a similar manner.

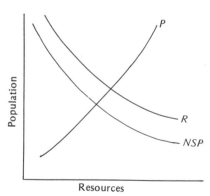

FIGURE 2.16   Resources (R), net societal product (NSP), and population (P).

Technology

Technology has often played a central role in cultural evolutionary theories. A wide range of postulated roles have been suggested for the influence of technology on culture change. These have ranged from autonomous technology as an energy manipulating variable, to the "leisure theory" of development. The latter theory suggests that technical innovations release labor from subsistence activities to participate in cultural activities. From a systemic ecological viewpoint technology is a limiting factor upon the production of goods and services and thus should be characterized by the types of inputs used, the output mix, and the quantitative relationships between inputs and maximum output.

Cultures, whether modern or prehistoric, must make a trade-off decision between two related but different input-output problems. On one hand, it is necessary for a culture to satisfy the material wants of the population using current technology and available limited quantities of natural resources, labor, and capital. This may be called the optimization problem which speaks to current needs with limited resources. On the other hand, it is also necessary to consider the developmental problem. A culture must increase its production through time in order to satisfy increasing demands which may either be the result of increasing population with the same demands or the same population with increasing demands or both.

The point where Peter robs Paul or the cause of the trade-off is if one invests scarce resources into future needs, (the developmental problem), one is diminishing the amount which is available for current needs, (the optimization problem). In other words, even with the same inputs, differing uses will change the amount of output through time.

Schumpeter's formulation of changing technology is used in our model. (see Chapter One). Schumpeter laid stress on "innovations" by which he meant either technological progress or resource discovery. In short, it is a change in the production function which brings about an increase in output. Although Schumpeter emphasized innovations both as a stimulus for disequilibrium and as the "mainspring" of autonomous investment, it is the former which is of interest in regard to our theory.

Accordingly, it is possible to start the analysis with the population and net societal product system in stable equilibrium. Development in the form of an innovation is the discontinuous disturbance of this equilibrium. The innovation may disturb the equilibrium by increasing production and output in the following three ways. First, it may render previous equipment obsolete. Thus, it raises the production costs while the new equipment replaces the old equipment. This may be and hopefully should be a short-term disturbance which should be compensated for by the greater efficiency of the new equipment. Second, it may create expectation of monopoly benefits in marketing or in the use of a new innovation, leading to investment in new production facilities. Third, the product or innovation is so attractive or valuable that demand for consumption increases and becomes larger than the value of labor. Thus, the household is willing to dip into savings in order to obtain the new product. This makes additional production necessary. In short, **the innovation is a change in the production function which brings about an increase in output through increased production. The increase in production output is the stimulus for the Malthusian disequilibrium.**

There are three other facets of the theory. First, significant innovations usually occur in clusters. A single innovation does not have a major effect upon production unless it is backed up by a series of reinforcing innovations. For example, the introduction of the internal combustion engine needed a vast number of reinforcing innovations, such as the expansion of highways and the petroleum and rubber industries, before the automobile industry caused an effective difference in the national product. Or, using a prehistoric example, irrigation had no long-term effect upon agricultural productivity unless the necessary social innovations took place allowing the maintenance of the canals, the distribution of water, and the allocation of the surplus product. Once a "cluster of innovations" has been introduced, they become a competitive necessity and diffuse widely.

Second, innovations require new institutions. Historically, Schumpeter argues that during the industrial revolution most innovations were produced and marketed by new firms. His reasoning, however, is more universally valid, namely, it is often more expensive to retool old production and marketing concerns than to produce new ones. Generalizing then, to other cultures—new innovations require new production and redistribution mechanisms which in turn require new social and economic institutions. Once the success of a new innovation is shown, there are groups of followers who are willing to attempt production and redistribution. This swarming effect includes the attempt to retool old industries and redistribution systems in order to meet changing patterns of demand. However, they are often at a competitive disadvantage due to increased cost of retooling.

Third, innovations are favored by the equilibrium state. The stability of the system results in minimal risk of failure while the small margin of resource surplus is the motivating force which results in the maximum pressure to innovate. As the intensification of the rate of innovation increases the disequilibrium of the net-societal-product population system, larger margins of surplus exist and the pressure for innovation decreases.

One reason why stability and equilibrium increases the rate of innovation is that the marginal efficiency or the marginal cost of investment is small. Thus, it is possible to argue that the cost of investment and the risk of failure are two causes for the innovation rate. If one puts these variables in a two-by-two table with the squares measuring rate of innovation, one would expect it might look like the following:

cost of investment ⟶

risk of failure ↓	high	medium
	medium	low

The rate of innovations

Figure 2.17 is a graphic representation of a cluster of Schumpeterian innovations in terms of their results on the net-societal-product curves.

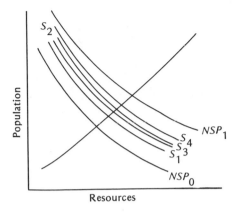

FIGURE 2.17 Schumpeter's innovations. This figure shows the increase in net societal product from NSP_0 to NSP_1 as caused by a "cluster of innovations," S_1, S_2, S_3, S_4.

Settlement Pattern

Before one may discuss alternative theories and methods behind the generation of settlement location, it is necessary to restate the model with zonal variables into a model with settlement variables. It is possible to define two variables: **settlement population** and **settlement threshold**. One may then apply the neo-Malthusian model to units of settlement as well as to zones.

The relationships among the settlement population, zonal population, and settlement threshold are that the population total for a particular zone is equal to the summation of all the populations within that zone, and the population of each settlement, no matter which zone, must be less than or equal to the settlement threshold which is the maximum population of a settlement. Where $P(I,J)$ is the population P of the Ith settlement in zone J; $PT(J)$ the total population of zone J; and ST the settlement threshold, these relationships may be stated as[3]

$$PT(J) = \Sigma P(I,J) , \qquad\qquad P(I,J) < ST .$$

The relationship among settlement population, zonal population, and zonal resources is that the population of any settlement in any zone must be less than or equal to the population total of the zone which it is in and both must be less than the net societal product (NSP) of that zone. Stated symbolically,

$$P(I,J) \leqslant PT(J) \leqslant NSP (J) .$$

In diagrammatic terms, this would be equivalent to adding a third line of settlement population curves beneath the zonal curves in Figure 2.10. In systemic terms the restatement is shown in the flow chart of Figure 2.18.

---

[3] In all the equations the notation is standardized so that the variable is subscripted in the following manner: $PT_J = PT(J)$.

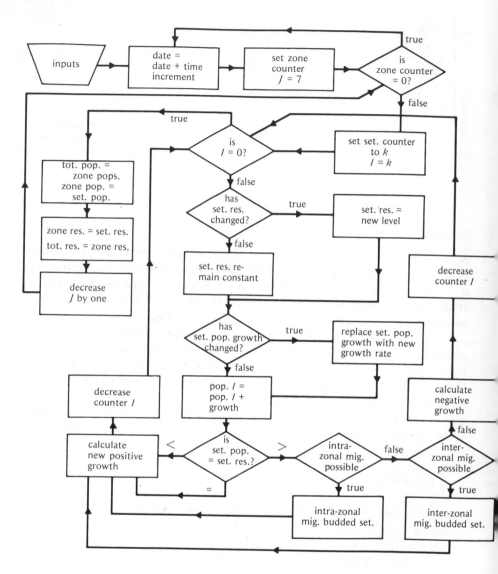

FIGURE 2.18   Restatement of systemic model in settlement terms—Systemic Model: Version 3. (pop. = population; res. = resource; tot. = total; set. = settlement; mig. = migration)

Settlement pattern classifications reflect the high degree of variability in both the settlement distributions and the theoretical problems for which the distributions are data. Thus, there are morphological classifications of rural and urban settlements (Dickenson 1964), size classifications (U.S. Census 1960), and functional classifications such as Christaller's central place hierarchies (1966). Critical, however, to all classifications is the central concept of location. If one conceptualizes settlement patterns in two-dimensional space, a simplifying assumption, it is possible to quantify the locational relationships. At one extreme are the regular patterns including settlements which are located in a line or in lattices. At the other extreme are the nonregular patterns, random distributions, clusters of settlements, or even single isolated settlements.

The problem which faces the model is twofold. First, what is the relationship between population and net societal product on one hand, and settlement location and settlement pattern on the other? Second, how may these relationships be operationalized? For the purposes of the model, it is assumed that once a settlement is located, it cannot be moved and still remain the same settlement. Settlements grow and die at the same location. If a settlement moves, for example, the Hano experience (Dozier 1966), it is similar to one settlement population becoming extinct and a new settlement being founded. **The simplifying assumption for the model is that settlement identity is equivalent to its unique location.** Thus, for new settlement formation to take place within the same resource zone, the population of a settlement must be greater than the settlement threshold and the zonal population total must be less than the zonal net societal product or symbolically,

$$P(I,J) > ST \text{ and } PT(J) < NSP\ (J)\ .$$

The size of the out-migrating population of a particular settlement in a particular zone is defined as the population of that settlement minus the settlement threshold. Symbolically, this equals $P(I,J) - ST$. This out-migrating population will form a new settlement. There are many factors which are involved in the choice of the new settlement location, of which three will be considered. First, the location may be randomly determined. Second, the location of new settlements may be determined by the location of other previous settlements and their relative population sizes. Third, the location of the new settlement is based upon the location of potential resources. In cases where the settlement population is greater than the settlement threshold and the zonal population is greater than the zonal net societal product, that is, $P(I,J) > ST$ and $PT(J) > NSP(J)$, it is possible to calculate the best zone for the migrants to locate. This is the zone with the smallest zonal population to net-societal-product ratio $[PT(J)/NSP(J)]$. With this information, the actual location within the new zone may be determined by any of the above three alternatives.

If one turns to the problem of operationalization, the choice of a random location may be determined by the use of a pseudo-random number generator or a random numbers table. In order to calculate the new settlement location on the basis of other settlements and populations, a population weighted "Bachi mean center of the distribution" is used (King 1969). For the third alternative, one may calculate the necessary resource area of existing settlement populations and locate the new settlement in that location which affords the best resource-population combination. For a more complete description of how these settlement locators operate, please see Appendix I.

THE COMPREHENSIVE THEORY

Social Organization

Variables such as spatial aggregation and population aggregation are indirect indices of social organization. Although related to settlement location they may be tested semi-independently of the simulation of the model. On purely theoretical grounds their relevance to the physical constraints on social organization may be argued from the following problem which assumes that the minimum possible organization is manifested in random behavior.[4] Imagine a box which has a group of balls moving randomly in the limited volume. If one diminishes the environment by making the walls of the box smaller and smaller—eventually the balls will form a lattice. Thus, one has caused a complex change in the motion of the balls from random to ordered behavior solely by decreasing the size of the environment which affects the activity of the internal components. An analogue often occurs when an elevator is loaded with people to its maximum legal capacity.

It is not difficult to substitute populations or settlements for the balls and a limited area such as a settlement or valley for the environment. At one level, if one begins to pack more and more people into a limited area defined by the boundaries of the settlement, it would begin to show more ordered behavior within its population. This would occur even if behavior of the population was originally random, which it is not. This phenomenon could be measured indirectly by the population aggregation (the number of people per settlement) in combination with the areal or volumetric size of the settlement (Ammerman, Cavalli-Sforza, and Wagner 1973). On another level, the decrease in the effective environment would cause settlement location in a region to be more ordered. For example, if part of a valley becomes noninhabitable, then a clustering of the settlements in the inhabitable portion is to be expected. This is possible to measure through the nearest-neighbor statistic which scales the relationship among dispersed, randomly distributed, and clustered settlements (Hagget 1966) or the "mean crowding" statistic which measures proximity (Lloyd 1967).

The cultural implications of the physical constraints on organization should be stated. Following Steward, it may be noted if there is a low density, highly dispersed population, there is little need for intergroup economic and social cooperation. However, as either population pressure forces multi-specialized zonal economies, or as environmental limitations take place, it becomes economically advantageous to develop reciprocity and redistribution systems. The latter is more efficient because: (1) distribution of goods becomes more dependable, (2) food failures at one settlement may be offset by the wider

---

[4] This problem is related to the "Ising problem" in physics.

joint resource base, (3) greater exploitation of the total resource base may take place through institutionalized intervillage specialization, and (4) a basis is provided for cooperation in other areas for such activities as construction and maintenance of simple irrigation systems (Johnson 1970).

From the above one may logically continue by using Durkheim's arguments of social solidarity and the division of labor (see Chapter One). Increasing population density brings greater specialization and increased division of labor. Increased division of labor brings a higher degree of social solidarity and social organizational complexity. Thus, from Steward's noncooperating, low density, highly dispersed, similarly employed population, there has developed a highly clustered, differentially employed, highly organized population. However, the population need not make the organizational shift, and one would expect the density to diminish.

Longevity

One of the major problems of settlement analysis is the question of longevity. Why does one settlement survive when a similar settlement fails? This problem is particularly difficult to analyze when there are sufficient resources to maintain both. There is insufficient information or theory pertaining to this question as is shown in a perusal of the literature on the cyclical nature of culture (Toynbee 1965; Willey and Phillips 1958), its decline (Eisenstadt 1967), or on cities (Mumford 1961; Dickenson 1964). For example, Willey attempts to explain the Postclassic depopulation of the Viru Valley in Peru with the exogenous factor of Chan Chan's greater resource and opportunity potential as a cause for differential settlement longevity (Willey 1966). A second example is provided by Rathje's argument that differential settlement extinction for the Maya decline is the result of differences in the import and export of goods and services (Rathje 1971). He claims that the core area trades social organization and services for raw resources from the peripheral areas. Although the demand for resources continues in the core area, the innovations in social organization and services become integrated into the societies of the peripheral area and thus the demand for core area commodities disappears. With the destruction of trade core area, settlements cannot exist, but peripheral area settlements survive.

McKenzie (1968) developed perhaps the most useful formulation of causes of differential settlement extinction applicable to the model which may be integrated into the concept of Schumpeterian innovation. He argues that, in an agricultural community, the point of maximum development is equivalent to an ecological climax. Thus, the community tends to remain in a balanced condition until a new element enters the system to disturb the status quo. This disturbing innovation, to use Schumpeter's term, acts in either a positive manner, resulting in growth, or a retractive manner resulting in emigration and readjustment to the circumscribed economic base.

The variable length of time that settlements exist must be accounted for. The model will attempt to use two alternative longevity functions. One might argue that under the conditions of decreasing resources longevity is a function of settlement size. A minimum population is necessary to keep a settlement in existence. This view is a simple extension of the population aggregation arguments suggested earlier. A larger settlement population can absorb a greater number of losses than a settlement with less population. If the amount of loss is constant over time and space or variable (but equally applied to both the larger and smaller settlements), it will take a longer time for the larger settlement to fall below the minimum level of settlement existence than the smaller settlement. It is important to note that if one is considering a rate of loss which is related to population size rather than the amount of the loss, the above argument does not hold and is thus not used as a longevity alternative.

The first alternative is based on MacArthur's belief that there is no population which is totally safe from extinction (MacArthur and Connell 1966). A finite probability exists that every settlement population will die. This probability is a function of existence and not of predation or competition. MacArthur has developed a measure of this probability, tk, which is the expected time for a population at its carrying capacity to become extinct if the population is not allowed to go beyond its carrying capacity. A population is considered relatively safe if the tk value is large and it is in danger of extinction if tk is small.

Instead of discussing the equation which appears in Appendix I, two other aspects of MacArthur's formulation can be noted here. First, the "time to extinction" is highly sensitive to the carrying capacity. A small change in the carrying capacity may magnify the change in the "time to extinction" by powers of 10. Second, the effects of predation (either inter-species or intra-species warfare for human populations) and competition, although both possibly resulting in extinction, do so through different mechanisms. The effect of predation is to decrease the growth rate or even make it negative by increasing mortality. Competition on the other hand, causes a decrease in the per capita carrying capacity or, in the terms of the model, the net-societal-product population ratio. The former increases the potential resources available to the surviving population; the latter decreases the potential resources. This contrast has clear implications for the use of highly predatory and exploitative policies by human populations faced with short-term stress.

This "time to extinction" alternative is applicable for determining longevity when the settlement population is near equilibrium or when there is a disequilibrium caused by population surplus with decreasing net societal product. The reader might argue that it is not appropriate for the MacArthur formulation to be applied to the population-surplus disequilibrium. However, after the population-surplus disequilibrium has begun to be corrected by an increase in the death rate, or, preferably, by emigration, the situation has returned to an equilibrium. Thus, unlike the growth disequilibrium, the decline disequilibrium may be examined as a set of diminishing equilibria in which the population is forced to diminish only when necessary. In the growth disequilibrium the population may grow for a period and not reach equilibrium, but in the decline disequilibrium the population is continually forced to decrease until the new equilibrium is attained due to the lack of resources.

The second alternative for determining longevity is based upon a random relationship which is calibrated to the actual data. For example, in the Hay Hollow Valley between A.D. 300 and A.D. 1450, there is a 1/10 probability that in any 100 years a site would become extinct. It is not difficult to adjust a pseudo-random number generator to simulate this 1/10 probability on the average. This does not argue that longevity is random, but gives a base line to measure its degree of deviation from randomness.

Climate

The rationale for isolating climatic factors is twofold. First it has been the most widely studied of the ecologically limiting factors (Boughey 1968). Second, palynologists such as Hevly (1970) and Martin (1963) and dendroclimatologists such as Fritts (1965) have developed considerable detailed data over long temporal spans for the Southwest. The climate is the summation of a large number of factors including temperature, moisture, radiation, light, air currents, and air pressure. However, a close interaction exists between temperature and moisture which in a large measure determine the faunal and botanical distributions. For example, using Holdridge's (1947) system of classification of world plant formation and life zones as a predictive device for the determination of major ecozones upon the Hay Hollow study area, one is able to make a set of predictions on the basis of altitude and mean precipitation (MacArthur and Connell 1966). The predictions that the study area is in a warm temperate latitudinal region, in a lower, upper altitudinal zone, in a semi-arid humidity province, and that it has thorn-scrub vegetation hold up when compared to the actual data. The Holdridge system predicts a mean annual biotemperature of 55°; the actual value is 51° based on a 37-year sample.

Climatic factors serve as a factor in resource growth for the theory and are calculated in the resource portion of the model. In other words, it will push the resource curves and the net-societal-product curves up or down depending upon whether the climatic conditions are favorable or unfavorable to biological growth.

Systemic Model—Version 4

Figure 2.19 is an abbreviated flow chart of the comprehensive systemic model incorporating all the factors discussed in the previous sections. It is the same as the simulation model and was prepared as part of the simulation for the testing of the model. The program was written in FORTRAN IV for use with an FORTRAN EXTENDED compiler. The model attempts to simulate carrying

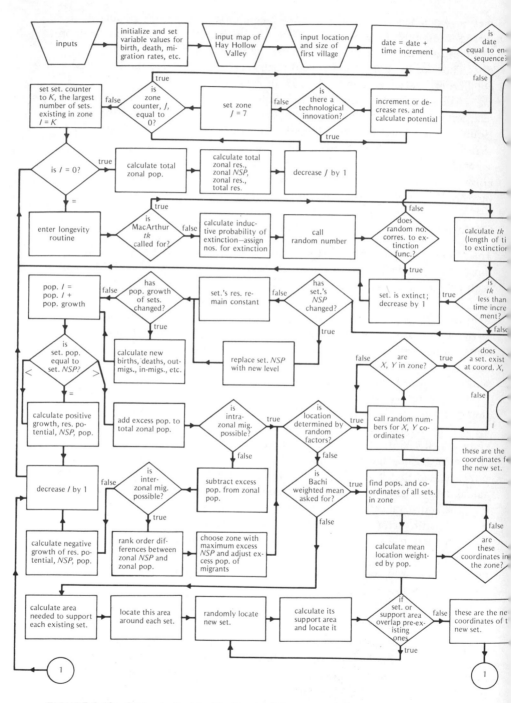

FIGURE 2.19 Systemic Model: Version 4. (pop. = population; res. = resource; set. = settlement; mig. = migration)

capacity as a dynamic equilibrium system. It originates with a small population in a single settlement. As time passes and ecological conditions change, the population grows and a budding process results in new settlements. The growth process continues until the settlements reach a maximum population. As resources diminish, the populations diminish and the settlements aggregate. Finally, they become extinct. The simulation is based upon four components: a population growth function, a population resource (NSP) check, a settlement locator, and a longevity function. The population growth function determines, at different birth, death and migration rates, how much the population grows through a given time span. The population resource (NSP) check defines the amount of resources which exist, the net societal product, and how much of the net societal product may be used at a particular level of technology following Schumpeter, and checks the population size against these limiting values. The settlement locator determines which zone and where in each zone new settlements will exist. Finally, the longevity function determines how long each settlement will exist for nonresource reasons discussed above. Thus, a population in a particular settlement may become extinct either for resource reasons which will be calculated in the population resource check, and or for nonresource reasons which will be calculated in the longevity function.

At the most simplistic level the four components fit together in the following way. The population growth component operates until the population resource check component shows that the population is too large for the zone. If it is not, the settlement locator locates a new settlement in the same zone as the original settlement and populates it with the excess population. If the total population is too large for the zone, the population resource check component calculates the best zone for the excess population and the settlement locator locates the site within that zone. Finally, the longevity function is called into play. If it causes a population to become extinct at a particular time, it resets the population growth function, the population check, and the settlement locator so that the settlement no longer exists. When resources in terms of usable net societal product diminish, the four components act in reverse to minimize the loss.

Actually, the systemic simulation model is more complex for these reasons. First, when there are multiple settlements growing in multiple zones and being checked against multiple resource levels, the number of possible variations and optimizations increases extensively, if not geometrically. Second, the population growth component and the population resource check component are defined by multiple equations and are not just single relationships. Third, the settlement locator and the longevity function components are both testing three alternative methods of determining the settlement location and two alternative methods of determining settlement longevity.

SUMMARY

A consideration of the anthropological, economic, and demographic literature in Chapter One provided a basis for a theoretical formulation of a systemic ecological model in Chapter Two that would be a productive approach to a study of long-term population growth. Most important in this theoretical review is the point that Malthusian and neo-Malthusian models have limitations when applied to short-term demographic studies particularly for societies whose technology has undergone the industrial revolution. However, there are strong arguments for neo-Malthusian models accurately representing long-term growth where the short-term masking effects may be differentiated from the long-term underlying processes in nonindustrialized societies. Thus, an ecological, neo-Malthusian model was developed which may be expressed graphically or systemically and was justified by and related to the major parts of relevant economic and demographic theory.

This model of carrying capacity as a dynamic equilibrium system was expanded from its simplified form by the addition of several variables and concepts. These variables and concepts include (1) spatial and temporal variations of resources, (2) migration, (3) population development at the zonal level, (4) various economic and demographic variables including the definition of the net societal product, (5) technology, examined from the basis of Schumpeter's theory of innovation clusters, (6) settlement pattern, (7) settlement longevity, and (8) climate. At various stages within the expansion of the model, the total model was expressed systemically to allow the reader to see the development and the increasing complexity of the system. The reader should turn to Appendix I to find a more specific discussion of the model including its quantification. The final systemic version of the comprehensive model is roughly the equivalent of the simulation model.

3

HYPOTHESES

Models provide a chance to test several hypotheses simultaneously. Scientific procedure suggests that one deduces a series of hypotheses from the assumption base of the model. Before examining the hypotheses and the deductions from which they are derived, one should note the most important considerations or criteria for the model's success. These are: (1) does the model successfully simulate reality? (2) is it useful heuristically for understanding the dynamic relationships between man, culture, and environment? (3) is it useful in showing the limitations of the data or theory upon which it is constructed? and (4) does it help produce new hypotheses? Here, the latter will be emphasized.

Deduction is a complex subject.[1] A deduction has a formal structure in which the explicandum, a formal conclusion, is a logically necessary consequence

---

[1] Archaeologists have been criticized for proclaiming the importance of deductive explanations without ever giving examples. There are two difficulties which are often not taken into account in these criticisms. First, most deductive explanations need a large number of definitions and assumptions spelled out in order to work. Second, there are many editors who do not see the value in what, at first glance, is repetitive formalization.

of the explanatory premises (Nagel 1961). A question which often arises is the priority of the premises, hypotheses, and deductions over the observations. This is not critical as long as the structure of assumptions, hypotheses, and observations hold together *ex post facto;* that is, none of the canons of logic or observation are violated in the formal analysis. However, this question of priority was a warmly debated issue in confrontations between the "new" and "old" archaeologists in the late 1960s and early 1970s. "Archaeology is an inductive science." "Archaeologists must observe real data or they are conjectural sociologists." "Archaeologists who don't manipulate ideas deductively are just field technicians tied to the chance of lucky prospecting." Any one of the above would have and did bring on arguments about the priority of ideas and data, deduction or induction.

A second question which adds to the complexity of deductions is whether a term may appear in the conclusion of a formal demonstration if it does not appear in the premises. In this study, the wider interpretation is used allowing new terms into the conclusion.

In Chapter Two, there was a consideration and graphical operationalization of the hypothesis that the development of population in marginal resource zones is a function of optimal zone population exploitation. This hypothesis may be deduced by formal syllogistic manipulations from the assumptions of the model and additional propositions.

There are two types of logical manipulation employed in this chapter; one is syllogistic; the other algebraic. The syllogistic form of deduction states that if a, then b; if b, then c; therefore, if a, then c. The algebraic form is the manipulation of a statement until it equals an identity or a truism. a is equal to b. b is equal to c. c is equal to a. Therefore, since a equals a, the system's logical consistency has been shown by identity.

Two advantages of formal deduction are apparent from the example below. First, the number of assumptions and propositions which are necessary to support a hypothesis is surprising. Second, the incompleteness of the hypothesis may become apparent. The original nondeduced hypothesis was incomplete insofar as it did not take into account that the development of marginal zone populations was not only a function of the optimal zone's population development, but of the total population.

The following is the verbal approximation and the formal deduction for the above hypothesis. (See Chapter Two, pages 29-30).

A. *Assumption:* The population of a resource zone is less than or equal to the net societal product. $PT(J) \leqslant NSP(J)$

  1. *Proposition:* The net societal product of a zone is a direct function of the resources of a zone. $NSP(J) = k[R(J)]$

2. *Proposition:*   The population of a zone is a direct function of the net societal product of a zone. $PT(J) = k[NSP(J)]$

3. *Conclusion:*   Therefore, the population of a zone is a direct function of the resources of a zone. $PT(J) = k[R(J)]$

    a. Definition: Resource zones, 1, 2, 3, are members of the set of resource zones. $\{R(J_1), R(J_2), R(J_3)\} \subset R(J)$

    b. Definition: Net societal products, 1, 2, 3, are members of the set of net societal products. $\{NSP(J_1), NSP(J_2), NSP(J_3)\} \subset NSP(J)$

    c. Definition: Populations, 1, 2, 3, are members of the sets of populations. $\{PT(J_1), PT(J_2), PT(J_3)\} \subset PT(J)$

4. *Proposition:*   The resources of zone 1 are less than the resources of zone 2 which are less than the resources of zone 3. Zones 1 and 2 will be called marginal to optimal zone 3. $R(J_1) < R(J_2) < R(J_3)$

5. *Conclusion:*   Therefore, the population of zone 1 is less than the population of zone 2 which is less than the population of zone 3. $PT(J_1) < PT(J_2) < PT(J_3)$.

6. *Proposition:*   The average population growth rate of a zone is equal to the population of the zone divided by the time it took to grow to the present size. $PG(J) = PT(J)/t(J)$

7. *Proposition:*   The time for potential growth in zones 1, 2, 3 is equal. $t(J_1) = t(J_2) = t(J_3)$

8. *Conclusion:*   Therefore, the average population growth rate of zone 1 is less than that of zone 2 which is less than that of zone 3. $PG(J_1) < PG(J_2) < PG(J_3)$

B. *Assumption:*   The summation of the populations of the zones is equal to the total population.
$$PT(J) = \sum_{J=1}^{n} P(J)$$

9. *Conclusion:*   Therefore, the population total is equal to the sum of the population of zones 1, 2, and 3. $PT = P(J_1) + P(J_2) + P(J_3)$

10. *Conclusion:*   Therefore, the population total is equal to the time for population development times the growth rates of zones 1, 2, and 3 summed. $PT = t[PG(J_1) + PG(J_2) + PG(J_3)]$

11. *Conclusion:*   Therefore, the development of the population in the marginal zones, 1 and 2, over time is a function of the development of the population in the optimal zone 3 over time and is a function of the total population. $PG(J_1) + PG(J_2) = -PG(J_3) + (PT/t)$

The second hypothesis to be deduced is that during periods of resource depletion, there will be a population aggregation of settlements.

A. *Assumption:* The population at a particular time is less than or equal to the net societal product at that time, which is less than or equal to the potential resources of that time. $P(t) \leqslant NSP(t) \leqslant R(t)$

1. *Proposition:* The net societal product of a particular time is a direct function of the resources of that time. $NSP(t) = k[R(t)]$

2. *Proposition:* The population at a particular time is a direct function of the net societal product of that time. $P(t) = k[NSP(t)]$

3. *Conclusion:* Therefore, the population at a particular time is a direct function of the resources of that time. $P(t) = k[R(t)]$

   a. *Definition:* Resources at time 2 and time 1 are members of the set of resources. $\{R(t_2), R(t_1)\} \subset R(t)$

   b. *Definition:* Net societal products at time 2 and time 1 are members of the set of net societal products. $\{NSP(t_2), NSP(t_1)\} \subset NSP(t)$

   c. *Definition:* Populations at time 2 and time 1 are members of the set of populations. $\{P(t_2), P(t_1)\} \subset P(t)$

4. *Proposition:* Resources at time 1, the earlier period, are greater than resources at time 2, the later period. In other words, a resource depletion is taking place. $R(t_1) > R(t_2)$

5. *Conclusion:* Therefore, the population at time 1 is greater than the population at time 2. $P(t_1) > P(t_2)$

   d. *Definition:* The population at a particular time is equal to the number of settlements at that particular time multiplied by the average settlement size at that particular time. $P(t) = n(t)[SP(t)]$

   e. *Conclusion:* Therefore, the population at time 1 equals the number of settlements at time 1 multiplied by the average settlement size at time 1. $P(t_1) = n(t_1)[SP(t_1)]$

   f. *Conclusion:* Therefore, the population at time 2 equals the number of settlements at time 2 multiplied by the average settlement size at time 2. $P(t_2) = n(t_2)[SP(t_2)]$

6. *Proposition:* The rate of population change (*ra*) is greater than the rate of settlement change (*rb*). $ra > rb$

   g. *Definition:* The population at time 2 is equal to the rate of population change times the population at time 1. $P(t_2) = ra[P(t_1)]$

   h. *Definition:* The number of settlements at time 2 equals the rate of settlement change times the number of settlements at time 1. $n(t_2) = rb[n(t_1)]$

7. *Conclusion:*   Therefore, the ratio of the population at time 2 to the population at time 1 is greater than the ratio of the number of settlements at time 2 to the number of settlements at time 1. $P(t_2)/P(t_1) > n(t_2)/n(t_1)$

8. *Conclusion:*   Therefore, the ratio of the number of settlements times the average settlement size at time 2 to the number of settlements times the average settlement size at time 1 is greater than the ratio of the number of settlements at time 2 to the number of settlements at time 1. $n(t_2)[SP(t_2)]/n(t_1)[SP(t_1)] > n(t_2)/n(t_1)$

9. *Conclusion:*   Therefore, the ratio of average settlement size at time 2 to the average settlement size at time 1 is greater than 1. $SP(t_2)/SP(t_1) > 1$

10. *Conclusion:*   Therefore, the average settlement size at time 2 is greater than the average settlement size at time 1. $SP(t_2) > SP(t_1)$

It may not be clear to the reader from Conclusion 10 that during periods of resource depletion, there will be a population aggregation of settlements. The above deduction shows that if resources at time 1, the earlier period, are greater than resources at time 2, the later period, then the average settlement size at time 2 is greater than the average size at time 1. In other words, as resources decrease, average settlement sizes increase showing the population aggregation of settlements. This is a combination of number 4 and number 10 of the deduction.

The hypothesis must be qualified, however, by number 6 in the deduction. The rate of population change is greater than the rate of settlement change. Since this proposition is reasonable, the hypothesis holds. To suggest the opposite would mean that a relatively small amount of population would be settling a relatively large number of settlements under resource depletion. This is a particularly inefficient strategy when one considers the increasing problems of labor allocation, resource allocation, and possible inter-village resource competition. These problems decrease efficiency and savings of scale which should be maximized for they have their greatest value during periods of resource depletion. Chapter Five includes a discussion of the more generalized hypothesis that population aggregation is inversely related to resources. There assumption 6 above is relaxed.

The third hypothesis to be deduced is that during periods of resource depletion, there is spatial aggregation of settlements. The deduction is similar to the deduction of the population aggregation hypothesis. Using the same general assumption and definition base, one may add the following statements to the previous deduction.

11. *Proposition:*   The rate of population change is greater than the rate of resource area change (rc). $ra > rc$

     a. Definition: The resource area (A) at time 2 is equal to the rate of resource area change times the resource area at time 1. $A(t_2) = rc[A(t_1)]$

12. *Conclusion:* Therefore, the ratio of the population at time 2 to the population at time 1 is greater than the ratio of the resource area at time 2 to resource area at time 1. $P(t_2)/P(t_1) > A(t_2)/A(t_1)$

13. *Conclusion:* Therefore, the ratio of the population to the resource area at time 2 (the population density of the resource area at time 2), is greater than the ratio of the population to the resource area at time 1 (the population density of the resource area at time 1). $P(t_2)/A(t_2) > P(t_1)/A(t_1)$

If the population, resources, and resource area are decreasing while the population density and average settlement size are increasing then the settlements must be aggregating spatially. This effect may be accurately measured by using one of several nearest-neighbor statistics such as the Getis statistic.[2] Nearest neighbor is more accurate than simple density since it allows one to distinguish aggregation even when density is decreasing. Finally, it should be noted that this hypothesis is qualified by two propositions, numbers 6 and 11.

    The fourth hypothesis to be deduced is that during periods of resource depletion, the residential area of sites decreases. In the following deduction one operates independently on both sides of the implication. This uses the previously discussed algebraic form rather than a syllogistic form of deduction.

Hypothesis: If there is a resource depletion between time 1, the earlier period, and time 2, the later period; then, there will be a decrease in the residential area (H) of the sites. $R(t_1) > R(t_2) \rightarrow H(t_1) > R(t_2)$

Proposition: The net societal product at a particular time is a direct function of the resources at that time. The residential area at a particular time is a function of the labor force (L) at that time since this limits residential construction. $NSP(t) = k[R(t)], \quad H(t) = k[L(t)]$

Proposition: The population at a particular time is a direct function of the net societal product at that time. The labor force at a particular time is a direct function of the population size at a particular time. $P(t) = k[NSP(t)], L(t) = k[P(t)]$

Conclusion: Therefore, if population at time 1 is greater than population at time 2, then population at time 1 is greater than at time 2 and the identity is proved. $P(t_1) > P(t_2) \rightarrow P(t_1) > P(t_2)$

---

[2] The Getis statistic is $c = (r_o - r_e)/\sigma r_e$ where $r_e = 1/2$ $\lambda 1/2$, r_o is the measured mean nearest neighbor distance, r_e is the standard error, and λ is the density of a Poisson probability function.

As has been noted in other sciences, there is a set of relationships between space and time. These relationships have been expressed in anthropology through the age-area hypothesis and most recently in archaeology through time-space systematics and in a quantifiable form in various articles by Deetz discussing the archaeological analogy to the Doppler shifts.[3] It is possible to replace in these hypotheses, the temporal variables with spatial variables and vice versa. Thus one produces new hypotheses (see Appendix II).

SUMMARY

Four hypotheses were deduced from the assumptions of the model of carrying capacity as a dynamic equilibrium system, as follows:

1. The development of population in marginal resource zones is a function of optimal zone population exploitation.

2. During periods of resource depletion, there will be a population aggregation of settlements.

3. During periods of resource depletion, there will be spatial aggregation of settlements.

4. During periods of resource depletion, the residential area of sites decreases.

All four of these hypotheses were deduced in such a way as to allow the reversal of the spatial and temporal dimensions without violating logical consistency.

---

[3] Archaeology is only one science which deals with time and space. Man's concept of the time-space continuum which contains elements common to the four deductions has been changed by the theory of relativity. In an often quoted statement, Minkowsky describes the results of this change. "From henceforth space in itself and time in itself sink to mere shadows, and only a kind of union of the two preserves an independent existence."

The history of any event will be represented in a space-time continuum as a continuous line which is called the world line. The same world line will determine for all observers the history of the event equally well. But each observer being in a different position or time will map that world line with slight or even large differences on the axes—three of space, one of time. Thus, the influence of the observer's motion, or different position in the space-time continuum, is shown through their choosing different axes of space and time. Thus, the continuum is both real and subjective—subjective insofar as the observer chooses the axes. The Lorentz transformation equations express mathematically the relationship between the different choices of time and space (Einstein 1921).

The relationship of time and space has been used by astronomers in estimating the age of the universe. The Doppler shift showing distances of ten billion light years also indicates that the universe is ten billion years old (Gill 1965). Wissler and many other cultural anthropologists and archaeologists have made rough use of this concept in the age-area hypothesis. The analogy has been made specific by Deetz who has shown that dating by seriation and rates of cultural expansion and contraction are dependent upon the location from which the analysis is done (Deetz and Dethlefson 1965).

4

DATA

INTRODUCTION

The Hay Hollow Valley (Figure 4.1) is located on the Navajo-Apache county line approximately twelve miles east of Snowflake, Arizona. Its latitude and longitude are 34° 34′, 109° 55′, respectively. Most of the valley is owned by the James Carter family and has been used as a cattle ranch.

This area lies near the border of the Anasazi cultural sub-area (located on the northern plateaus of the four corners of Utah, Colorado, Arizona and New Mexico) and the Mogollon cultural sub-area (located in the southeastern part of the Southwest). The Anasazi tradition dates from B.C. 100 (Basketmaker II) through A.D. 1700 (Pueblo IV). The Mogollon is divided into five phases which also begin about B.C. 100 and ends approximately A.D. 1500.

For the past fifteen years the valley, as well as the Little Colorado River drainage, has been the location of intensive archaeological work directed by   53

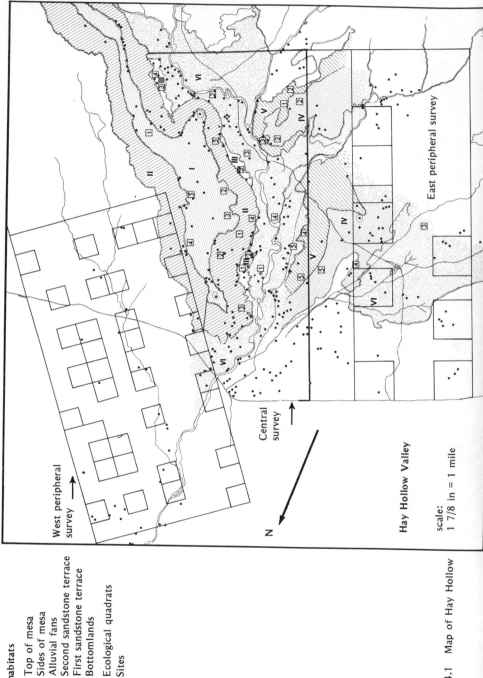

Microhabitats

I   Top of mesa
II   Sides of mesa
III   Alluvial fans
IV   Second sandstone terrace
V   First sandstone terrace
VI   Bottomlands
□   Ecological quadrats
•   Sites

West peripheral survey

East peripheral survey

Central survey

N

Hay Hollow Valley

scale:
1 7/8 in = 1 mile

FIGURE 4.1   Map of Hay Hollow
Valley.

Paul S. Martin of the Chicago Field Museum and his students. A considerable amount of information about the prehistory and paleo-anthropology of this Anasazi-Mogollon transitional area has been obtained and published in several volumes of the Fieldiana Anthropology series, six dissertations, and many articles in professional journals. As it continues to be an area of intense research, there will most probably be more publications by the time this study appears.

Following is an outline chart of the major prehistoric occurrences in Hay Hollow Valley as they were understood in 1970. Although other materials have also been used, this outline is primarily a combination and updating of William A. Longacre's "A Synthesis of Upper Little Colorado Prehistory, Eastern Arizona" (1964), and John Johnson's "Settlement Systems and Cultural Adaptation in the Hay Hollow Valley, A.D. 950-1100" (1970).

BRIEF OUTLINE OF HAY HOLLOW PREHISTORY

Phase 1

Concho Complex: B.C. 1000-A.D. 200.   In this first phase the procurement of food primarily involved the collection of wild game and plants with occasional horticulture.

The sites reveal small, nonpermanent camps containing fire and storage pits. There is no evidence of architecture.

It has been inferred that the social organization consisted of localized, unilateral, exogamous groups and that nuclear families lived in single domiciles.

Phases 2 and 3

Incipient Agriculturalists and Initial Sedentary Agriculturalists: A.D. 200-750. There was an increasing dependence on agriculture for most of this period. However, based on quantified tool kits, hunting and gathering still predominated as a subsistence strategy. However, from evidence based on tool variation, the growth in agricultural dependence reversed after A.D. 500.

Small pithouse villages were found consisting of one to five houses which were associated with storage pits. After A.D. 500, villages were usually located near arable land. Beginning in A.D. 450, there was a trend toward greater dispersion of habitation sites which approached a hexagonal pattern toward the end of this period. Yet, up to A.D. 600, the size of the villages remained quite homogeneous.

The social organization was similar to that of Phase 1. However, there was a decrease in social distance and autonomy after A.D. 500 and little intersite complexity up to A.D. 600.

This phase marks the first appearance of pottery at approximately A.D. 500. The major types are Alma Plain, incised, and neckbanded, and San Francisco Red wares.

The size of the population increased up to A.D. 500 but started to decline about A.D. 600.

Phase 4

Established Village Farming: A.D. 750-900.   Between A.D. 750 and 800 agriculture became the predominant subsistence factor.

There were large pithouse communities of five to fifteen houses each, indicating greater site aggregation. The sites began to redisperse after A.D. 850.

During this phase prior to A.D. 850, none of the villages appear to contain more than two family groups. The increasing aggregation of villages reflected the development of intersite social clustering. This can be measured through the stylistic attributes of the pottery. However, with the redispersion of the settlements, there was also increasing economic and social autonomy.

Black-on-white decorated pottery first appears with White Mound and Red Mesa types. Alma Plain and Scored, Forestdale smudged, Lino gray, Lino Black-on-gray, and San Francisco also appear.

The population decreased until A.D. 800 and then, with the predominance of agriculture, started to increase.

Phase 5

Beginnings of Planned Towns: A.D. 900-1100.   Agricultural dependence decreased until A.D. 1050 (Leone 1968). However, this is not documented by one analyst (Burkenroad 1968). At approximately A.D. 1000 irrigation first appeared in the valley and it may be responsible for the sudden rise in agricultural dependence after A.D. 1050. It has been shown that by A.D. 975-1000 the population was greater than could have been supported by rainfall agriculture.

By the end of this period pueblo architecture ranged from small rectangular shapes to plaza oriented towns with distinct religious structures, i.e., kivas (usually a cluster of settlements will contain one with a great kiva). There was a general proliferation of sites as a result of "budding off" processes. Because of the exploitation of optimal zones, these new sites were located in the more marginal ecological zones. Thus, there was an increased density of sites whose pattern across space when considered as a whole was close to random.

Inter- and intra-site complexity increased with 44% of the sites representing more than one local group. Indeed, the larger sites have been demonstrated to contain multiple matrilocal residence units in one village. There are various indications of intersite social organization and possible redistribution centers. These include the scope of irrigation and the clustering of sites grouped around "nuclear centers."

The pottery styles are Snowflake Black-on-white, Showlow Black-on-red, Wingate Black-on-red, and various corrugated forms.

This is the period of maximum population growth which culminates in A.D. 1025 according to one authority, although probably later according to others. After the peak was reached, there was a rapid decline.

Phases 6 and 7

Established Towns—Beginning of Convergence and Large Towns—Full Convergence: A.D. 1100-1450.   An environmental shift and a population surplus produced a strain in the resource potential. Thus, there was decreasing resource potential per capita for production. This may have been partially and temporarily offset by the savings of scale which were a result of the greater cooperation possible in aggregated villages with larger populations. However, there are fewer sites and the total population was smaller than in the previous period. There was a shift to greater dependence on wild plants. After A.D. 1200, the village dependence on agriculture decreased.

There are large masonry pueblos with kivas, great kivas or plazas, or both. These settlements tend to be located on the edge of the optimal ecological zones as a result of the aggregation of population as shown by the high average number of rooms per site.

This was the period of maximum intra-site complexity indicating integration within communities. However, a breakdown in regional organization is suggested by the decrease in intersite complexity. This would correspond to the increased number of uxorilocal residence units that have been demonstrated at Broken K Pueblo by James Hill (1970).

Four Mile polychrome, St. Johns polychrome, Snowflake Black-on-white, and various brown corrugated and textured pottery forms appear.

Population declines with final abandonment coming between A.D. 1350-1400.

For detailed information on materials summarized here the reader is directed to the following articles in the bibliography: Burkenroad 1968, Cook 1970, Gregory 1969, Hevly 1970, Hill 1970, Johnson 1970, Klein 1969, Leone 1968, Longacre 1964 and 1970, Martin *et al.* 1964, Martin and Fritz 1966, Plog 1969, Schiffer 1968, and Zubrow 1970.

SURVEY DATA

It is critical to any prehistoric demographic study to obtain a broad areal understanding of archaeological resources through the use of surveys. The Hay Hollow Valley and the Little Colorado River drainage area have been the scene of six surveys of variable intensity. Of these, three are significant for this study.

In 1967, the "central" portion of the Hay Hollow Valley covering an area of 5.2 square miles was surveyed.[1] This is marked Central Survey in Figure 4.1.

---

[1] A brief statement about the survey technique is *apropos.* After maps and aerial photographs of the survey area were gridded, a crew of five to ten members of the expedition would cover an individual grid unit by walking back and forth across the area in a line approximately five yards apart. Thus, the area was covered not only systematically but completely.

In this survey 100% of the area was systematically covered on foot in order to estimate the size of prehistoric population, the duration of occupation, and the variety of adaptive strategies. All sites were recorded that were defined by the explicit criterion that any spatially unique sherd, lithic, or architectural cluster was a site. In order to acquire a site designation, the clusters had to be surrounded by areas of noncultural materials and could not be the result of possible redeposition by water or by pot hunters. Samples of the cultural materials were collected from the surface of each site. In the 100% survey, 277 sites were found of which 198 were datable using the surface pottery collections.

In 1968, two peripheral survey areas were defined to measure the amount of spatial and cultural variation. One survey was east and the other was west of the 100% sample survey. These are labeled the East and West peripheral survey on Figure 4.1. Both of these surveys were 25% samples. The same type of on-foot surveying was continued and the same criterion for the definition of sites was used. The datable sites were dated by Paul Martin in the 1967 and 1968 surveys on the basis of pottery.

There are several parameters which need to be considered in taking survey data and converting it to archaeological data. First, one must estimate the room counts of those sites which have not been excavated. Fred Plog calculated two linear regression equations which inductively related room number to sherd scatter and room block area. This was based on the relationships which existed in known excavated and surveyed sites in the area.[2]

A second parameter is the relationship between total room count and the number of habitation rooms.[3] It is likely that there is a gradual increase in the ratio of nonhabitation to habitation structures through time. This reflects the increased material benefits resulting from a rising standard of living brought about through technological and social innovations. To take this into account, population estimates would have to be lowered through time by an increasing factor. This has been done by using several ratios based inductively on known sites such as Carter Ranch and Broken K (Plog 1969; Schiffer 1968; and others).

One must also consider a third parameter—how many of the habitation rooms were occupied at one time? This was calculated by taking 80% of the habitation rooms at the midpoint of the site's duration (Plog 1969; Schiffer 1970).

---

[2]   The equation for pithouse villages is $R = .114 A + 1.2$ where R is the number of rooms and A is the area in square meters of the sherd scatter. The equation for pueblos is $R = .10 B + .4$ where R is the number of rooms and B is the area of the room block in square meters (Schiffer 1968).

[3]   For a discussion of functional determination of rooms from surface remains see Zanic (1968).

As previously mentioned, the valley has been divided into topographic and potential ecological zones (or microhabitats) numbered I-VI. Each surveyed site was located within these zones. Topographically, these are (I) the top of the mesa, (II) the sides of the mesa, (III) the alluvial fans at the bottom of the mesas, (IV) the second sandstone terrace, (V) the first terrace, and (VI) the bottomlands (see Figure 4.1).[4] The exact environmental composition of these potential microhabitats will be discussed later in this chapter. The survey data then consists of a complete listing of surveyed sites by site number; their spatial locations; their pottery, C-14, pollen, or tree-ring dates,[5] or the resource zone in which each site was located; and the total number of rooms, the maximum number of rooms occupied contemporaneously, and the number of habitation rooms for each site.

Two caveats should be noted. First, because the data was compiled by many people over the last eight years, inconsistencies have crept into the data which are not correctible without extended field work. For example, one archaeologist has site number 506 located within the sample square, but the map drawn by another originally shows the site outside the sample square.

The second caveat is that the data were often compiled for different problems in mind and thus the degree of completeness within the data varies somewhat. Perhaps these caveats are an argument for having a single person gather and analyze the data for a single problem. However, in large projects this is often unfeasible because as the field rapidly grows interests and relevant problems change. Furthermore, these data were gathered as part of the Southwest Archaeological Expedition which is a field school devoted to teaching research as well as field methods. In a sense the goal of educating students who must analyze the data conflicts with the goal of achieving consistency in data. Despite these problems, the record does show a remarkable set of data, that is, 405 located sites, of which 313 are datable, 326 are located in their resource zone, and 134 are habitation sites in which the number of rooms, number of habitation rooms, and maximum number of contemporaneously occupied rooms have been calculated.[6] This is represented in a short form here in Figure 4.2 which shows a three-dimensional histogram representing the distribution of the number of rooms across the space of the Hay Hollow Valley, that is, the number of rooms located at a particular area. This data is equaled in only a few other archaeological areas by data with comparable representative qualities.

---

[4] Zone VI is the same as VI and VII in Zubrow (1971).

[5] The pottery date is based on surface collections as given at the time of the survey by Paul S. Martin except in cases where the site was excavated prior to 1969. In those pre-1969 excavated cases where C-14, tree-ring dates, or pollen dates caused a reanalysis of the site date, the amended date was used (Zubrow 1971).

[6] For a complete listing of the data site by site one should see *A Southwestern Test of An Anthropological Model of Population Dynamics* (Zubrow 1971).

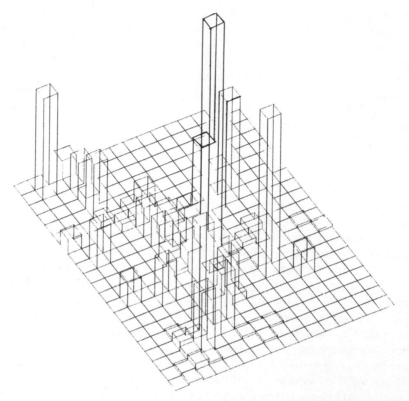

FIGURE 4.2   Histogram showing the Hay Hollow population distribution. Vertical axis represents the population and the two horizontal axes represent the actual spatial locations as on a map.

INTENSIVE SURVEY

In the summer of 1969, an intensive survey of seven sites was undertaken to determine and compensate for the following inadequacies of the surface surveys. In the use of surface indications one may overestimate what is under the ground. Also, one cannot establish accurate dates solely from surface pottery collections. More accurate data were necessary than were available for testing some of the hypotheses, such as the residential area hypothesis. In addition, a primary question when using survey materials is whether or not one may estimate multi-component sites, that is, a site which has been occupied at two distinct time periods (for example, A.D. 300-500 and A.D. 800-900). In the process of surveying, several questionable sites were found, and it was necessary to check them more carefully. Finally, several sites were being pot hunted extensively and it was decided to collect as much data as possible in the context of the ongoing research and then attempt protection before total destruction had taken place.[7]

The intensive survey was utilized on New Survey (NS) sites 83, 137, 195, 196, 201, 430, and 511, which were not chosen randomly nor should they be considered representative. They were chosen for multiple criteria, one of which was that they emphasized areas of possible dating and size error. The sample was skewed to maximize the potential error between the previous survey estimates and what actually occurred underground. Thus, any major problems in the original survey estimates could be detected. Within this set of sites, NS 83 and NS 137 were chosen because there were reasons to believe that they might be multi-component sites. NS 511 was included because it was thought to be the latest site in the valley. The rest of the sites were selected because they were near access roads and previous archaeological work and they were beginning to be pot hunted extensively. In fact, each site had at least one pot hole in it and some had considerably more damage.

The intensive survey was carried out in a series of steps. First, the site was relocated in the field and checked against aerial photographs and existing maps. Second, a new surface collection of the pottery remains was made. Third, the site was analyzed for surface features. Fourth, the topsoil of approximately one to two inches covering the top of the walls was removed and the architectural layout was mapped. Fifth, in problematical areas, trenches were put in to clarify the architectural features of the site. Sixth, pottery collections tree-ring specimens, C-14, and pollen samples were taken from the exposed floor area. Seventh, a bulldozer and a small front-end loader were employed to gather soil from nonarchaeological areas surrounding the site which was then placed upon the site providing a three- to five-foot sterile protective cap.

In no case was more than 11% of a site's room blocks and interior plazas excavated. In some sites it was possible to use existing pot holes. Figure 4.3 (a-g) shows the maps of the seven sites which were extensively surveyed. Table 4.1 is a comparison of the actual number of rooms as determined from the in-

---

[7] One of the unfortunate consequences of maintaining a long-term research interest in a particular area is that the value of the area becomes known to local pot hunters. An expedition such as the Southwest Archaeological Expedition, which has been located in the same area for fifteen years, becomes a part of the local society and economy, and its work and personnel are discussed in the same manner as the work and personnel of the local industries, such as lumber or cattle. At the same time, the expedition itself, in an attempt to maintain good relations with the owners of the land and the local population, had attempted to publicize the value of the area's archaeological resources and the reasons why they should be excavated by professionals. However, it appears that the expedition failed somewhat in its attempts to dissuade local pot hunters. In the four summers in which I was associated with the expedition, pot hunting increased. Not only did many of the habitation sites have pot holes in them, but recently heavy machinery was used. At Broken K, plow and furrowing machinery were used in the burial area to find graves even though the owners of the land have attempted more than once to keep unauthorized people off their property. At Four Mile ruin, a nine yard front-end loader was used to remove the burial area of the site in an attempt to find whole pots.

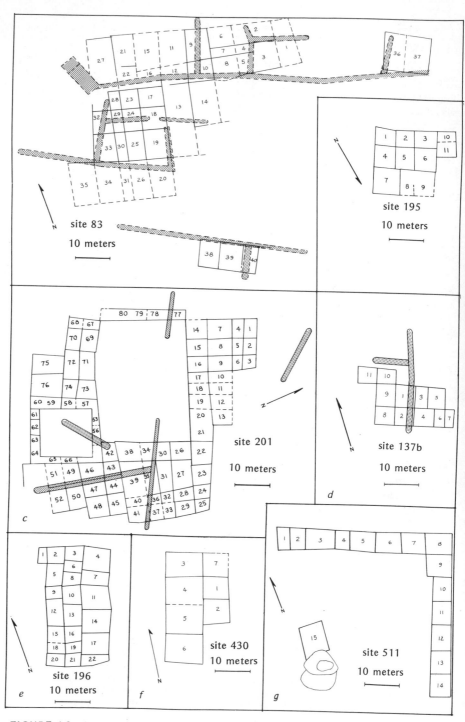

FIGURE 4.3   Intensive survey sites.

Table 4.1.   Comparison of settlement sizes.

New survey site number	Intensive survey— actual number of rooms	Surface survey— estimated number of rooms
83	43	25
137	10	20
195	11	25
196	22	1
201	76	20
430	7	20
511	14	14

tensive survey with the estimated number of rooms for the original 1967-68 surface surveys. The intensive survey shows an average of 26.1 rooms per site compared to the 17.8 rooms per site of the 1967-68 survey.

Three conclusions may be drawn from these data. First, and most importantly, the original survey does not overestimate the number of rooms, in fact, it may underestimate the number. Second, remembering that the sites were chosen for maximum potential error in the estimation by survey techniques, it is clear that the survey estimates for such "problem" sites taken individually cannot be trusted since the range of the error is too great.[8] The best estimate, NS 511, had no error while the worst, NS 137, had a −200% error. Third, when taken as a group, there is a tendency for those sites which are overestimated to be compensated by other sites that are underestimated. Thus, the difference between the averages for the "problem" sites is only 8 rooms. The actual error for typical sites is probably considerably lower, about 15%.

Each of the sites was dated by pollen dating and on the basis of pottery. Six of the seven sites were also dated by C-14. (Unfortunately, there were insufficient funds to run more than one date per site.) Table 4.2 shows the pollen dating, Table 4.3 shows the C-14 dating, and Table 4.4 shows the pottery counts and dates. The three sets of dates are compared graphically in Figure 4.4. A final date estimation was made on the basis of maximum overlap shown as the vertical lines on the graph. These are the overlap dates. Table 4.5 compares the original survey dates with the overlap dates.

First, the 14 intensive survey dates and the 14 estimated survey dates were averaged separately. Then the average estimated date was subtracted from

---

[8]   The percentage of error was calculated as:

$$\% \text{ error} = \frac{\text{Intensive Survey } - \text{ Surface Survey}}{\text{Intensive Survey}}$$

Table 4.2   Pollen dates of intensive survey sites from Hay Hollow Valley.[a]

New survey site number	Pollen sample Number	AP/NAP[b] Ratio	Dates
201	1-6	Low AP	650-925; 975-107! 1150-1300
83	7-11	Insufficient pollen	
137b	12-13	Increased AP	575-625; 925-975; 1075-1150+; 1300
195	14-16	Low AP	650-925; 975-1075 1150-1300
511	17-18	Increased AP	575-625; 925-975; 1075-1150+; 1300-
430	19	Increased AP	575-625; 925-975; 1075-1150+; 1300-
196	20-22	Low AP	650-925; 975-1075 1150-1300

[a] Compiled by Richard H. Hevly.
[b] AP = arboreal pollen; NAP = nonarboreal pollen.

Table 4.3.   Carbon-14 dates.

New survey site number	Geochron laboratory number	Date	Range
83	Gx-1661	930 ± 85	845-1015
195	Gx-1660	1155 ± 85	1070-1240
196[a]	Gx-1664	690 ± 90	600-780
137	Gx-1662	710 ± 95	615-805
201	Gx-1665	1360 ± 90	1270-1450
430	No C-14 dates run		
511	Gx-1663	990 ± 80	910-1070

[a] The carbon material for this sample was taken from a fire pit 20 feet outside of the pueblo and may not be associated with it.

Table 4.4. Pottery types of intensive survey sites.[a]

Pottery type	83	137b	New survey site number 195	196	201	430	511
Snowflake Black-on-white	x	x	x	x		x	x
White Mount Black-on-white		x				x	
Red Mesa Black-on-white		x				x	
St. Johns Black-on-red							x
Show Low Black-on-red, exterior corrugated	x			x			
Show Low Black-on-red	x		x	x	x	x	
Wingate Black-on-red				x	x		x
San Francisco Red		x					
Alma Plain				x			
Plainware							x
Lino Gray		x		x			
Four Mile Polychrome							x
St. Johns Polychrome			x	x	x		
Querino Polychrome				x			
McDonald Painted Corrugated	x	x	x	x	x		
Corrugated - Plain	x	x	x	x	x	x	x
Corrugated - Indented	x		x	x			
Painted ware - no design elements					x		
Black-on-white - no design elements		x		x		x	x
Unidentifiable			x	x			
Estimated dates A.D.	850-1300	900-1000	1150-1250	1150-1250	1125-1250	1000-1100	1300-1400

[a] compiled by David Gregory.
[b] 137b has a pithouse village component which may influence this pottery distribution.

the average intensive survey date. This calculation shows that the average difference between the dates for all the sites is only 40.0 years. If one excludes NS 137b, which is a multi-component site having both pithouses and a small pueblo, there is only a 11.6-year difference. If one excludes NS 137b and NS 83, which is also possibly a multi-component site, there is a 43.5-year difference. We can thus conclude that (1) the estimated survey dates are remarkably close to the intensive survey dates and thus may be accepted as reasonable and (2) that the multi-component specific sites such as 137b and possibly 83 produce very poor estimates. Thus, no single dating estimate should be given a great deal of reliance unless one has evidence that the site is *not* a multi-component site.

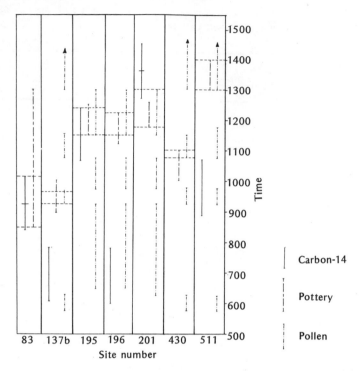

FIGURE 4.4 Comparison of pottery, pollen, and carbon-14 dates for intensive survey sites. Horizontal lines indicate where dates from the different techniques overlap.

Table 4.5. Comparison of settlement dates (A.D.).

New survey site number	Intensive survey date	Estimated 1967-68 survey date
83	300-1025	1100-1300
137	930-970	500-700
195	1150-1240	1000-1200
196	1150-1225	1100-1280
201	1175-1300	1100-1200
430	1075-1100	1000-1150
511	1300-1400	1200-1450

Since the intensive survey shows that the data from the other surveys are reliable (noting the above caveats), the latter were used to test the hypotheses, model, and theories.

ECOLOGICAL DATA

Introduction

During the summer of 1970 Richard Hevly and I directed an ecological survey for three reasons. First, we wanted to determine if the topographic and soil zones corresponded to differences in flora and fauna. If so, were these differences sufficiently great as to be labeled different microhabitats or resource zones? Second, we wished to determine the actual amount of resources and resource productivity available to the prehistoric population. Third, we wanted to obtain these resource figures with sufficient representative accuracy so they could be used in the simulation of a model of carrying capacity as a dynamic equilibrium system.

The ecological survey consisted of the following eight stages:

Stage 1 was the accurate determination of the topographic and soil zones.

Stage 2 involved the plotting and field location of a representative sample of nested quadrats in each potential microhabitat for floral analysis.

Stage 3 was the plotting and field location of a series of representative transects for each potential microhabitat for faunal analysis.

Stage 4 was the initial gathering of floral data.

Stage 5 was the gathering of animal data.

Stage 6 was the final gathering of floral data.

Stage 7 was the planting and harvesting of three plots of corn.

Stage 8 was the relating of modern resource data to past resource data.

Stages 1, 2, and 3

Attempts were first made to determine microhabitats in the Hay Hollow Valley by Schacht in 1968, who used U.S. Geological Survey aerial photographs to differentiate two major ecological zones—a highland zone with juniper pinyon and a lowland zone predominant in saltbush grasslands. He then differentiated two geographic and edaphic zones within the highlands. The western highlands had soils derived from basalt, while the eastern highlands had soils derived from shale. Topographically, he divided the western highlands into the mesa top (zone I) and the mesa sides (zone II), while the eastern highlands were divided into an upper (zone IV) and lower (zone V) terrace. The lowlands, although not divided on geographic or edaphic criteria, were divided topographically into upper (zone III) and lower (zone VI) bottomlands. Schacht felt but was unable to demonstrate that zones I and II and zones IV and V might differ only in minor details.

Minor corrections in Schacht's original formulation were made using a new set of aerial photographs from the Strategic Air Command, which had a much finer degree of detail and resolution than the USGS photographs, and using detailed soil maps of the area from the U.S. Soil Conservation Service. Most of these corrections dealt with the boundaries of zone IV and V and the boundary of zone III. The corrected version is shown in Figure 4.1.

We decided to take a series of floral and faunal samples from each of the potential microhabitats to provide us with the quantified data necessary for the statistical differentiation of the actual present day microhabitats. These samples would also allow us to quantify the actual present day resource potential of the microhabitats. One might object to this procedure as having no relevance to the past. Two answers are possible to this objection. First, although one probably would not want to suggest that the floral samples from today are exactly equivalent to those of the past, they do give a reasonable estimate. In fact, they are far more accurate than the generalized archaeological statements about the environment which one finds in the literature. Second, it is possible to relate the modern environment and floral samples to the past by using such environmental indices as palynology (see the discussion of stage 8 below).

A series of problems had to be solved before it was possible to know that our floral samples were representative. Line transects are the easiest and quickest sampling procedure for estimates of density, frequency, and cover. However, there was some question whether line transects would give an accurate estimate of the plant material. In this case, due to the aggregation of plants in small areas, we decided to test the relationship between transect versus quadrat data on trees. We did this by sampling ten areas, each of which consisted of four nested quadrats with four different size transects, each having a 90° angle. It was found that in all cases this method seriously underestimated the number of trees, showing average errors for each transect as −65%, −34%, −33%, and −22%.

A second sample was taken in order to test if line transects selected on a criterion of at least two trees in the first 30 meters gives a more accurate and representative estimate. This method was also rejected for the error is even greater than the first method with average errors of −79%, −41%, −44%, and −46% for the four different size transects, respectively.

Having rejected both line transect methods, it was decided to attempt the use of quadrats as a sampling method in two new samples. The question arose as to what was the smallest quadrat which would give valid representative data but which was small enough to be handled by the expedition's resources? It was assumed that if a quadrat gave an accurate representation of the number of trees in an area of more than an acre, it was representative and sufficiently accurate. The largest quadrat, 68 meters square, is more than an acre; the smallest is 1/16 of the largest; the next largest is 1/4; and the next is 9/16. The errors were 101%, 20%, and .4% for 17-meter square, 34-meter square, and 51-meter square, respectively for the quadrats of the first sample, and 72%, 31%, and 10% for same size quadrats of the second sample.

It would appear that the quadrats are capable of producing better estimates. However, it should be noted that in order to make accurate estimations it takes a far larger quadrat size than the professional biologists and ecologists usually deem necessary. For example, Smith (1966) claims:

The size of the quadrat must be adapted to the characteristics of the community. The richer the flora, the larger or more numerous the quadrats
must be. In forests, quadrats of one fifth acre are established to include
the trees, while smaller quadrats can be used to study shrubs and understory. For the latter as well as grass cover, quadrats of one square meter
are the usual size.

In other words, for rich flora such as forests one should not have to use quadrats of more than one-fifth of an acre. Hevly (1970) notes that common nested quadrat sizes are 10 meters square for trees, 4 meters square for shrubs,
bushes, and understory, and 1 meter square for grasses. Since these values are
based on larger studies where quadrat size was correlated with many more than
60 quadrat estimates, we decided that it would be appropriate to compromise
our large quadrat size with professional values. Thus, we decided to use quadrats of 30 meters square for trees, 12 meters square for shrubs, bushes, and understory, and 1 meter square for grasses. Five of these were randomly located
in each potential microhabitat and their exact location is plotted in Figure 4.1.
However, it should be noted that this size quadrat may have built-in errors up
to 25%.

In order to determine the amount of faunal life, a series of road transects
were devised which cut across the potential microhabitats. We also used live
trapping.[9] These methods were chosen primarily on the basis of logistic ease
and time requirements rather than on statistical or sampling reasons.

Since animal data are quite variable, the longer the transect, the more accurate is the relative representation of the population. The greater the isolation of the transect, the less disturbance of the fauna but the greater the logistic problems resulting in a shorter transect. Thus to maximize the length
of the transects, they were taken along already existing roads. It may be argued that the automobile traffic along these roads would result in a skewed
sample. However, during prehistoric times there was a sizable population in
the valley and the animal distribution would also have been affected by human
activity. Therefore, the skewed samples may be approximately equivalent. Also, the skewing is considerably less than what might be expected since the
roads along which the transects were taken have very little traffic, averaging
from one automobile every four hours to one automobile every two months.

Stage 4

This stage was the initial gathering of the floral data. The number and size of
trees were derived from the 30-meter-square quadrats, the number and size of

---

[9]   These are just two of many potential methods which could have been used. Smith
(1966) suggests sample plots, strip census, mark-recapture method, the population remov-
al method, live trapping, and pellet counts as alternative methods. Each of these has
assets and disadvantages.

bushes and shrubs were derived from the 10-meter-square quadrats, and the number and size of the herbs and grasses from 1-meter-square quadrats. The data were collected in a manner which allowed us to determine the number of the plants per nested quadrat per microhabitat. Table 4.6 shows the summation of the number of plants derived from the five groups of three nested quadrats in each potential microhabitat.

Table 4.6.   Total plant distribution for all quadrats by microhabitat.

Species	Number of plants in all quadrats in microhabitat					
	I	II	III	IV	V	VI
Trees						
Pinyon Pine		9		1	3	
Juniper	29	131	26	70	55	1
Shrubs						
Saltbush *(Atriplex)*	2	2	8	1	9	30
Sagebrush *(Artemisia)*	15	40	8	61	22	
Prickley Pear *(Opuntia)*	8	19	13	7	6	5
Cholla *(Opuntia)*	13	1	3	2	1	4
Barberry *(Berberis)*			2		3	
Winter Fat *(Eurotia)*	4		1			24
Yucca *(Yucca)*	1		9	1	2	
Beargrass *(Nolina)*						3
Other: Lycium	4		3			1
Berberis		1				
Ephedra		1		7	1	
Echinocenis		1	1			
Amorpha			1			
Forestiera			1			
Cliff rose				9	13	
Ironwood					3	
Herbs						
Grass: *Aristida*	12		15	1		
Agryopyron		6				
Bouteloua	334	61	34	14	12	92
Hilaria					33	
Muhlenbe Gia	19	1	35	19	3	1
Sporobolus		35	33	20	10	65
Other: Aster	35				1	
Boerhaavia				2		
Goosefoot *(Chenopodium)* red mist	1					
Snakeweed *(Guteriezia)*		15		1	1	3
Buckwheat *(Eriogonum)*				2		
Locoweed *(Astragalus)*			1		2	
Other: Plantain	1					
Artemisia wormwood			4			
Sphaeralceo			1		1	
Cryptantha					5	14
Aster						8

In order to determine the reality of the zones two tests were made. First, a chi-square test was done using the sum number of each species for the five quadrats in each microhabitat. The observations thus formed a matrix of 35 species by six microhabitats. The resulting chi-square was significant at greater than the .0001 level. Thus, one may conclude that the six microhabitat distributions taken as a group show the result of factors other than chance variation as well as being a group independent of each other *vis a vis* the distribution of plants.

The second test was done to tell if there were significant relationships between the individual microhabitats when analyzed one against the other rather than as a group. In order to do this a series of Pearson Product Movement Correlation coefficients was run between the various microhabitats. High significant values of the correlation coefficients indicate that there are similar proportions of the various species of plants in the two microhabitats being correlated. The correlation coefficients using the sum data are in Table 4.7. By sum data I mean that the cases are the total number of plants of one species in the five nested quadrats in a microhabitat. The italic values are the significant ones. If one uses mean data rather than sum data the correlation coefficients are as in Table 4.8. By mean data, the mean number of plants of one

Table 4.7. Correlation coefficients of total number of plants by species by microhabitat using sum data.

Microhabitats	I	II	III	IV	V	VI
I						
II	*.42*					
III	*.49*	*.69*				
IV	.16	*.85*	*.54*			
V	.17	*.80*	*.41*	*.78*		
VI	*.66*	.31	*.55*	.09	.11	

Table 4.8. Correlation coefficients of numbers of plants by species by microhabitat using mean data.

Microhabitats	I	II	III	IV	V	VI
I						
II	*.43*					
III	*.49*	*.61*				
IV	.16	*.81*	*.54*			
V	.16	*.80*	*.41*	*.78*		
VI	*.68*	.31	*.55*	.08	.08	

species for the five nested quadrats in a microhabitat are the cases. It is interesting to note the high degree of similarity between the two sets of correlation coefficients even to the extent that they have identical combinations which are statistically significant. From these correlation coefficients it is possible to conclude that microhabitats II, IV, and V have a high degree of similarity. The square of the correlation coefficient, r^2, is considered to be a measure of the amount of variability explained. Therefore, r^2 for microhabitats II-IV, II-V, and IV-V is .66, .64, and .61, respectively. This means that 66% of the variability in microhabitat IV is explained by microhabitat II. The other values explain the variability for II-V and IV-V in the same manner. These microhabitats show the highest degree of similarity of all the microhabitat combinations. It seems reasonable to conclude on the basis of correlations whose values are approximately .80 that the three microhabitats show sufficient similarity so as to be called one microhabitat. This is, of course, solely on the basis of floral data.

Stage 5

Stage 5 was the gathering of animal data from the transects and from live trapping. Each transect covered a width of 1/10 mile. The area total of the transect in each potential microhabitat is:

microhabitat I	1.380 square miles
microhabitat II	.144 square miles
microhabitat III	.110 square miles
microhabitat IV	1.650 square miles
microhabitat V	.544 square miles
microhabitat VI	3.054 square miles
microhabitat VII	6.900 square miles

Microhabitat VII is a continuation of potential microhabitat IV towards Snowflake.

Tables 4.9 and 4.10 are the summation of the transect data and also include the density data which were calculated by dividing the summation data by the potential microhabitat areas. Pearson Product Movement Correlation coefficients were calculated on the density data by potential microhabitats. Table 4.11 shows only one significant correlation of sufficient size that suggests two potential microhabitats, IV and VII, are the same animal microhabitats. Since microhabitat VII is a continuation of microhabitat IV, it is not surprising that the two zones correlate sufficiently so as to be described as essentially the same microhabitat. Using the r^2 value, both II and IV explain approximately 72% of the variability of each other.

What is interesting is that unlike the floral microhabitats, zones I-VI do not correlate with each other sufficiently to be able to combine any of them into one microhabitat. Thus, we have four floral microhabitats and seven faunal microhabitats. This difference should have settlement dispersion consequences in that during the periods of hunting and gathering economies there should be a greater dispersion of sites across the microhabitats.

Table 4.9. Total animal transect data.

Animals	I	II	III	IV	V	VI	VII
				Microhabitats			
Mammals							
Deer	2						
Antelope	1						1
Cottontail rabbit	3			2	6	1	
Jack rabbit				1	4	1	
Coyote						2	
Squirrel	2	1	1	1		1	6
Gray fox	1						
Reptiles							
Lizard (collared)	1	1		2	2	1	
Lizard (striped)					3		
Snake						1	
Horn toad	1						4
Other lizards				2		1	
Large insects							
Bug						1	
Fly	2			1			
Bee		7	2				
Grasshopper	11				2	5	
Butterfly						1	
Moth							
Dragon fly						1	1
Cicala	1						
Snails	1						
Birds							
Hawk, night	7			1	1		
Buzzard, Vulture	5	1		1		6	3
Raven	1			17		1	3
Crow	2		1			1	2
Jay	30	1		2			2
Dove	1			21	4	13	19
Says Phoebe	2	1		13			6
Flycatcher	5	1		7		3	6
Mockingbird	17		1	3	8	23	14
Meadowlark	1			13		6	
Sparrow, Vesper	1			47	1	4	75
Sparrow, Brown	20	3		52	7	5	33
Barn Swallow							1
Cliff Swallow							4
Other Hawks	1					2	
Red Tail Hawk			3			1	
Sparrow Hawk							3
Towee	1						
Black and White Warbler							3
Speedbird	1			1			1
Towns Tanager	1			1			
Thrashers							4
Peewee				1			3
Blackbird				3			3
Owls							1
Orioles				3			
Plain Titmouse					6		
Kingbird				3		1	
Other and unknown	26	5		25	11	10	49

Table 4.10.   Total animal transect data by density per square mile.

Animals	I	II	III	Microhabitats IV	V	VI	VII
Mammals							
Deer	1.4						
Antelope	.7						.1
Cottontail rabbit	2.2			1.2	10.8	.3	
Jack rabbit				.6	7.2	.3	
Coyote						.6	
Squirrel	1.4	6.9	9.1	.6		.3	.9
Gray fox	.7						
Reptiles							
Lizard (collared)	.7	6.9		1.2	3.6	.3	
Lizard (striped)					5.4		
Snake						.3	
Horn toad	.7						.6
Other lizards				1.2		.3	
Large insects							
Bug						.3	
Fly	1.4			.6			
Bee		48.6	1.8				
Beetle							
Grasshopper	8.0				3.6	1.6	
Butterfly						.3	
Moth							
Dragon fly						.3	.1
Cicala	.7						
Snails	.7						
Birds							
Hawk, night	5.1			.6	1.8		
Buzzard, Vulture	3.6	6.9		.6		2.0	.4
Raven	.7			10.3		.3	.4
Crow	1.4		9.1			.3	.3
Jay	21.7	6.9		1.2			.3
Dove	.7			12.7	7.2	4.3	2.7
Says Phoebe	1.4	6.9		7.8			.9
Flycatcher	3.6	6.9		4.2		1.0	.9
Mockingbird	12.3		9.1	1.8	14.4	7.5	2.0
Meadowlark	.7			7.8		2.0	
Sparrow, Vesper	.7			28.5	1.8	1.3	10.9
Sparrow, Brown	14.5	20.8		31.5	12.6	1.6	4.8
Barn Swallow							.1
Cliff Swallow							.6
Other Hawks	.7					.6	
Red Tail Hawk			27.3			.3	
Sparrow Hawk							.4
Towee	.7						
Black and White Warbler							.4
Speedbird	.7			.6			.1
Towns Tanager	.7			.6			
Thrasher							.6
Peewee				.6			.4
Blackbird				.6			.4
Owls							.1
Orioles				1.8			
Plain Titmouse					10.8		
Kingbird				1.8		.3	
Other and unknown	18.8	34.7		15.1	19.9	3.3	7.1

Table 4.11.   Correlation coeffcients of animal densities by microhabitat.

Microhabitats	I	II	III	IV	V	VI	VII
I							
II	.42						
III	.01	−.01					
IV	.38	.31	−.09				
V	.58	.35	.02	.43			
VI	.47	.15	.17	.35	.63		
VII	.38	.32	−.03	.85	.47	.42	

A hunting and trapping expedition was directed by Richard Hevly in September in which both vertebrates and invertebrates were collected from three areas termed habitats. Habitat 1 was zones IV and V; habitat 2 was zones VI and III; and habitat 3 was zones I and II. Two sets of results from the vertebrate survey are relevant. First, the similarity coefficient run on trapped animals per species per habitat show that the three habitats are distinct, thus agreeing with the transect results. Second, since the animals were trapped and weighed, it was possible to determine the amount of vertebrate biomass that each of these three habitats is capable of supporting (see Table 4.12).

The original species by species tabulation shows that for invertebrates the grassland and pinyon juniper woodland are easily distinguished from each other but both share a complement of species with the juniper savanna.

Thus to summarize on the basis of ecological quadrat and transect data, there are four floral microhabitats and seven faunal microhabitats. The trapping data show clear demarcation of the three tested habitats for vertebrates.

Table 4.12.   Amount of trapped biomass by habitat.[a]
             Distribution expressed in grams per square meter.

	Habitat		
	Pinyon juniper woodland 1	Grasslands 2	Juniper savanna 3
Vertebrate species	6	11	6
Carnivores	.003	.033	.004
Herbivores	.091	.327	.102
Invertebrate species	17	23	16
Carnivores	.01	.05	.05
Herbivores	.025	1.05	.95

[a] Compiled by Richard Hevly.

However, for invertebrates there is similarity between one habitat and each of two distinct habitats.

Stage 6

The size of the standing crop was determined to evaluate the potential resources. Each of the 1-meter-square quadrats whose species tabulations make up part of Table 4.6, was clipped during stage 4, and a sample of the species making up the 10-meter-square quadrats was also clipped. These clippings were weighed by genera per quadrat per potential microhabitat. The summation of the floral results are the following:

microhabitat I	70.7500 ± 10.2971 g/m^2
microhabitat II	36.9900 ± 2.6608 g/m^2
microhabitat III	26.6060 ± 11.8317 g/m^2
microhabitat IV	24.2020 ± 9.9155 g/m^2
microhabitat V	42.4650 ± 12.6035 g/m^2
microhabitat VI	62.3460 ± 7.8297 g/m^2

Adding the results of the vertebrate and invertebrate survey to the floral standing crop, it is possible to determine the total standing crop for each potential microhabitat as follows:

microhabitat I	71.856 g/m^2
microhabitat II	38.096 g/m^2
microhabitat III	27.066 g/m^2
microhabitat IV	24.556 g/m^2
microhabitat V	42.819 g/m^2
microhabitat VI	62.806 g/m^2

In no zone is the faunal biomass more than 2.9% of the total biomass, and for all zones it averages 1.5% of the total biomass. This indicates that an economy heavily dependent on fauna would be severely limited. In fact, it would be even more limited if the relative food values of the faunal biomass to the floral biomass are calculated. Using the 4 kcal/g for floral biomass (Odum 1966) and the 2.16 kcal/g for faunal biomass derived from food composition tables, one finds that the relative food value of the fauna is only 8% of the flora.

From the above, one could rank the ecological zones from highest to lowest carrying capacity I, VI, V, II, III, IV. However, this is somewhat misleading. The size of the standing crop influences the capacity to produce but it is not the actual capacity to produce. An analogy is capital in a bank. The capital influences how much is produced but the actual production is the result of capital and the interest. The productivity is the amount of renewable growth which is similar to interest payments. As long as the capital or standing crop stays the same one may drain off interest payments or productivity amounts without affecting the capital or standing crop. Similar structures may be suggested for subsistence economies based on carrying capacity systems as may be suggested to the banker who is looking for long-term gains with minimum risk, that is, don't dip into your capital.

To determine the productivity of the potential microhabitats, the same 1-meter-square quadrats were reclipped one month later. These second sets of clippings were also weighed by genera per quadrat per zone. The results were:

microhabitat I	10.0800 ± 2.1513 g/m^2
microhabitat II	12.4000 ± 2.7746 g/m^2
microhabitat III	14.6600 ± 2.3986 g/m^2
microhabitat IV	7.1800 ± 4.2247 g/m^2
microhabitat V	2.1400 ± 0.8640 g/m^2
microhabitat VI	22.7000 ± 13.7340 g/m^2

It is important here to note that the productivity figures do not exactly correspond to the total standing crop figures. In other words, because potential microhabitat I has the largest standing crop does not mean it has the largest productivity. Potential microhabitat VI has the largest productivity. Unfortunately, the study was not in the field long enough to gather data on animal productivity.

Stage 7

To estimate the amount of production possible from agriculture, three plots of corn were planted. Two were planted in microhabitat VI and one in microhabitat IV. One of the two plots in microhabitat VI was located on "dry" land near the Gurley site. The only source of water was rainfall and runoff. The other plot was located near a water-filled irrigation ditch. The same method of planting was used in each of these sample plots. The grass was cleared for an area of three feet in circumference around each hole in which the corn was to be planted. Then a one-foot-diameter hole about six inches in depth was dug. Into each hole was put 15-20 kernels of variegated, red, green, and yellow Hopi corn. In each of the microhabitat VI plots, five holes were dug and around one hole a protective screening was placed. Each hole was watered and then covered.

The third plot of corn was planted in Mrs. Carter's garden in microhabitat IV. Here two half-rows of corn were planted by pushing the corn kernels into the turned soil. Mrs. Carter watered and weeded this plot.

The results of this experiment were ambiguous at best. No corn whatsoever grew in the microhabitat VI plot near the irrigation ditch and only one corn plant grew in the "dry" microhabitat VI plot. The plot which was grown in Mrs. Carter's garden resulted in a full crop producing approximately the same amount of corn as the modern hybrid species which are being grown both in that garden and the surrounding area. Calculating then solely on the basis of modern conditions for the county and using food composition it is possible to produce 25.43 g/m^2 of corn kernels which is equivalent to 91.29 kcal/m^2. This must be considered as productivity since corn is an annual plant. Comparing the corn productivity value with the total natural floral productivity value of the most productive microhabitat, microhabitat VI, it is important to note that 91.29 kcal/m^2 is only 1.01 kcal greater than the 90.28 kcal/m^2 of the natural flora. This clearly raises the question of why do agriculture? The answer may lie in the relative expenditure of energy necessary to get the 90 kcal under different forms of subsistence or in the fact that not all of the floral productivity is humanly consumable. Of course it must be remembered that the present day types of corn are far more productive than prehistoric corn. However, this data may suggest that the change from gathering to agriculture need not be a major quantum leap in productivity or standing crop.

Stage 8

Stage 8 is an attempt to relate the modern environment to past environments. As James Schoenwetter has pointed out, this is the most difficult and tenuous part of palynology because it is impossible to determine the environment quantitatively and accurately from the pollen rain. It is complicated by six factors (Butzer 1964). First, there is differential representation of pollen due to differing surface receptivity and differential preservation of pollen under different environments. Second, there may be under- or over-representation of species due to small or excessive pollen production, insect pollination, or easily decomposed pollen. Third, there is documentation of long distance transport of pollen by the wind which sometimes exceeds 100 km. Fourth, there is possible redeposition of pollen from older sediments. Fifth, pollen is transported by streams. Sixth, pollen sequences are often truncated or incomplete due to fire destruction of sections, and interruptions or lateral distortion in the sedimentation process.

To quantitatively determine the previous biomasses from the present biomass two parameters must be established. First, for a base line, one needs to find at what time in the past the present biomass existed. Second, one needs to determine the amount of fluctuation around this base line. The important assumption is made that if the modern pollen rain is equivalent to past pollen rain, then the biomasses at both times are equal, and changes in external factors such as climate affect the microhabitats about equally.

Pollen spectra have been constructed and arranged in chronological order from floors of sites in the Four Mile, Shumway, and Hay Hollow Wash archaeological areas (Hevly 1964). Figure 4.5 is a copy of this spectra modified to show which areas are most similar to the modern day environment. These periods are A.D. 275-350, A.D. 1100-1200, and A.D. 1350-1400, and are the baseline figures on which the modern environment will be mapped for comparison.

In order to determine the amount of fluctuation two factors will have to be considered. First, Hevly concludes on the basis of a wide group of pollen spectra that:

> The fluctuations do not appear to be random or significant variation of arboreal pollen but can be shown to be more or less synchronous over a wide area. Such changes may represent fluctuation of vegetation zones by as much as 500 feet suggesting that movement of zones similar to that documented historically in southern Arizona may have been occurring for many millenia (Hevly 1964:113-114).

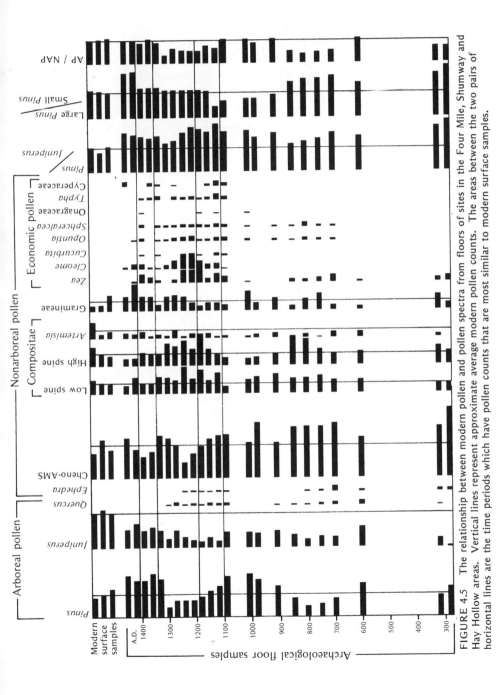

FIGURE 4.5   The relationship between modern pollen and pollen spectra from floors of sites in the Four Mile, Shumway and Hay Hollow areas. Vertical lines represent approximate average modern pollen counts. The areas between the two pairs of horizontal lines are the time periods which have pollen counts that are most similar to modern surface samples.

This factor of 500 feet fortunately happens to be the difference in altitude between both microhabitats VI and III and microhabitat I. This difference then may be considered the maximum difference not for two microhabitats but for any one microhabitat through time. It is now possible to put the parameters on resource change through time. Using microhabitats I and III the change in standing crop limit is 44.1440 g/m^2 and in productivity is $-4.58g/m^2$. If one uses microhabitats I and VI the change in standing crop over time is 8.404 g/m^2 and in productivity is -12.62 g/m^2.

Figure 4.6 is the pinyon pine pollen profile from the valley which Hevly considers to be the most sensitive independent monitor of moisture and temperature, that is, the pinyon pine production is minimally affected by man. Setting the modern day environment at A.D. 300 from the combined pollen chart, one may reasonably suggest that in 800 years, that is, the peak of the pinyon pollen, the standing crop increased a maximum of 44.1440 g/m^2 and the productivity -12.62 g/m^2.

To put this in perspective, these figures allow us to quantify the change through time of the standing crop and productivity of the microhabitats. This has numerous advantages. For example, we will be able to use real resource data as a parameter in the simulation of our model when considering the consumption of resources by the population.

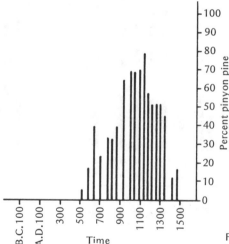

FIGURE 4.6 Pollen profile from the Hay Hollow Valley.

SUMMARY

After an updating of the known archaeological record from the Hay Hollow Valley, four major areas of archaeological data were discussed: excavations, a 100% central survey, two 25% peripheral surveys, and an intensive survey. The intensive survey was done to test the validity of the archaeological data. In particular, it was necessary to show that the dating and the site size from the surveys were accurate. Three conclusions drawn from the intensive survey were that (1) the original survey underestimated the room count, (2) the survey dates were remarkably close to the intensive survey dates and thus may be accepted as reasonable, and (3) the multi-component sites produced poor temporal estimates when surveyed.

An ecological survey was conducted to determine the reality of potential microhabitats and to determine the actual amount of resources and resource productivity available to the prehistoric population. This survey showed the reality of the potential microhabitats of which four were floral and seven were faunal. Floral productivity, standing crop data, and faunal standing crop data were obtained. The quantified resource data were related to past resources through the pollen sequence. It was suggested that the development of agriculture was not as significant a shift in production as has been generally assumed.

5

TESTS OF HYPOTHESES

To what extent do the data of Hay Hollow Valley support the hypotheses presented in Chapter Three? In a sense, if the data support the hypotheses, they will also support the model. This is analogous to the way the positive test of a series of theories supports a paradigm (Kuhn 1968). Just as the theories have been deduced from the assumptions of a paradigm, the hypotheses have been formally deduced from the assumptions of a model. Thus, the question which this chapter will attempt to answer is to what extent do the data support our hypotheses and model?

FIRST HYPOTHESIS

The original formulation of the first hypothesis stated that the development of population in marginal resource zones is a function of optimal zone population exploitation. After the formal deduction it was found necessary to restate this **83** hypothesis as follows: the development of the population in the marginal zone is a function of the development of the population in the optimal zones and a function of the total population. The essential difference between the two statements of the hypothesis is the addition of the variable of total population. In order to test the first hypothesis, two independent tests were made. The first utilizes the archaeological population indices from the Hay Hollow Valley, while the second estimates the actual carrying capacity values. The results of both tests must be compared to the predictions of the model.

The operationalization of the original first hypothesis and the test implications for the population indices were discussed in Chapter Two in the section entitled "Migration and Population Development at the Zonal Level" (pp. 27-30) It was shown there that the predicted population curves by zone would be similar to Figure 2.13, if the resource curves were constant over time. If, however, the resource curves should drop at a particular point in the temporal sequence, the resulting carrying capacity decrease would result in larger out-migration from the system or increased mortality. The latter possibility was diagrammed in Figure 2.14.

One would expect the resource curve of microhabitat VI to be the highest solely on the basis of its density of the present flora and its proximity to water resources. Microhabitat VI would reflect the highest carrying capacity and would deserve to be labeled the optimal zone of the study universe. The other zones may be labeled marginal. Figure 5.1 shows the number of habitation rooms in the central 100% sample. The general similarity of the shapes of the curves in Figures 2.13, 2.14, and 5.1 are clear. One may use the total number of sites, as in Figure 5.2, as an index of population. This index clearly shows a greater similarity to Figure 2.14 than to Figure 2.13. Two conclusions should be drawn from these comparisons. First, the data substantiate the hypothesis insofar as the actual curves follow the predicted curves of the relationship between the optimal and marginal zones. Second, these results indicate that there is a change in the population distribution caused by a decrease in the carrying capacity after A.D. 1150 or, in the terms of the model, a decrease in the resource curves.

This decrease has been explained as the result of a change in effective moisture caused by a change in the seasonal rainfall pattern at approximately A.D. 1150 (Schoenwetter and Dittert 1968). Hevly (1970) explains this decrease in resources with multiple factors including a change in rainfall pattern from summer dominant to winter dominant or to a biseasonal pattern, and a change in the temperature pattern from warm to cool.

It is clear, however, that the changing resource curves or carrying capacity should be verified independently of the model and the population indices of the valley. As was discussed under stage 8 in Chapter Four, a series of pollen analyses were undertaken. The pinyon pollen which correlated to a high degree with agricultural and gathered economic pollens is the most sensitive monitor of moisture and temperature. Thus, the change in pinyon pollen is a

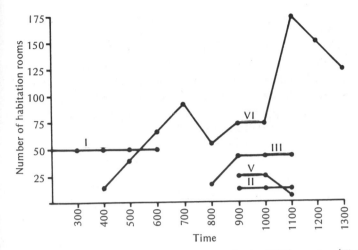

FIGURE 5.1   Number of habitation rooms in the 100% sample. (There were no rooms in microhabitat IV.)

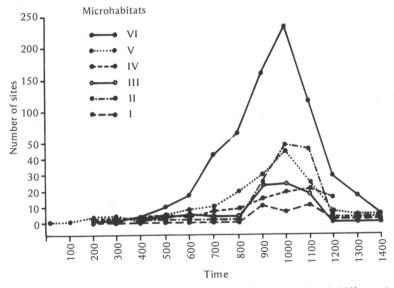

FIGURE 5.2   Total number of sites in the 100% sample and both 25% samples.

relative index of the change in the resource curves (Figure 4.6). The pinyon pollen curve independently shows that there was a drop in the resource curves after A.D. 1150 as moisture decreased and temperature increased.

The second test of the first hypothesis involves the estimation of carrying capacity and population values from zonal resource data. On the basis of predicted migration pattern (Figure 2.12), one would expect that the zonal ordering of the population sizes would follow the amounts of zonal resources particularly when both resources and population are at a maximum. Before the ecological data were collected in 1969, an attempt at estimating carrying capacity was made (Table 5.1). The area of each microhabitat was calculated from aerial photographs and maps. Somewhat arbitrarily, the amounts of dry grams of biomass produced were taken from Odum's values for agriculture and arid areas. It was assumed on the basis of the United Nations world sample of nutrition that 2500 kilocalories per day were necessary and sufficient to maintain an average individual in the population. Consumption was estimated arbitrarily but reasonably at 5% of the total produced biomass. (As long as one is interested in the relative ordering of the zonal population estimates, rather than the actual amounts of population, the size of the consumption figure is irrelevant if it is applied equally across space and time.) Examining Table 5.1, one would expect the population size to decrease by potential microhabitats in the following order: VI, V, III, IV, II, I.

Since the areal figures of Table 5.1 include both land covered in the 100% central and both 25% peripheral samples, one must use Figure 5.2 to test the validity of the simulated microhabitat ordering. Here, the actual distribution of sites by microhabitat when resources and population are at a maximum are VI, II, V, III, IV, I. Only microhabitat II is out of the expected sequence of decreasing population sizes.

The possible reasons for this sequence discrepancy also point out some of the simplifying assumptions in this original estimate: (1) that Odum's values were reasonable, (2) that the sites were located in the same microhabitat which they utilized, (3) that the geographic size of the microhabitats remained constant over time, and (4) that there was no attempt to define multiple microhabitat utilization per site (Zubrow 1971).

It is now possible to relax the first assumption. Table 5.2 presents data based on the ecological survey reported in Chapter Four, without the use of Odum's values. The first part of the table includes the area of the microhabi-

Table 5.1.   Maximal carrying capacity values derived from Odum's estimates of biomass.[a]

	I	II	III	IV	V	VI
			Microhabitats			
Area of the zone in mi.^{2}	1.17	2.15	.92	1.43	2.84	9.92
Biomass in g/m2/day	.3	.2	.5	.4	1.0	2.0
Kcal/g biomass	4.0	4.0	4.0	4.0	4.0	4.0
Population based on 5% consumption and 2500 kcal per person	70	80	190	120	290	4110

[a] Zubrow 1971.

Table 5.2.   Maximal carrying capacity values using ecological data.[a]

	I	II	Microhabitats III	IV	V	VI
Zonal Distributions						
Area of the zones in mi^2	1.17	2.15	.92	1.43	2.84	9.92
Floral standing crop in g/m^2/day	2.36	1.23	.89	.81	1.42	2.08
Floral productivity in g/m^2/day	.34	.41	.49	.24	.07	.76
Vertebrate standing crop in g/m^2/day	.053	.053	.180	.047	.047	.180
Invertebrate standing crop in g/m^2/day	1.0	1.0	1.1	.26	.26	1.1
Total known biomass in g/m2/day	3.753	2.693	2.660	1.357	1.797	4.120
Population at 5% Consumption						
Population based on floral standing crop	572	549	169	239	833	4272
Population based on floral productivity	84	184	93	71	42	1555
Population based on vertebrate standing crop	13	24	34	14	28	370
Population based on invertebrate standing crop	242	445	210	77	153	2261
Population based on total known biomass	911	1202	504	401	1056	8458

[a] Zubrow-Hevly.

tats in square miles, the floral standing crop, the floral productivity, the vertebrate fauna standing crop, the invertebrate fauna standing crop, and the total known biomass all in grams per square meter per day. The second part of Table 5.2 presents the number of people that could be supported using the floral standing crop, the floral productivity, the vertebrate standing crop, the invertebrate standing crop, and the total known biomass. It is interesting to note the size of the discrepancy between the amount of population capable of being supported by invertebrates in comparison to vertebrates. On the average, the invertebrates are capable of supporting ten times as many people as the vertebrates. It would seem reasonable to suggest that the role of invertebrates has been often underestimated.

On the basis of Table 5.2, using the last row, one would expect the population sizes to decrease by microhabitats in the following order: VI, II, V, I, III, IV. Comparing this with the sequence of actual distribution of sites by microhabitat when resources and population are at a maximum (Figure 5.2), once again one microhabitat is out of sequence, this time microhabitat I, not microhabitat II, as previously identified by using Odum's values.

This discrepancy in expected and observed values for microhabitats I and II may be partially explained by the change in subsistence patterns. These microhabitats, because of the steepness of the slope and their location on the point of the mountain, would provide the most difficulty in the use of the major sources of water. Since agriculture became the primary form of subsistence after A.D. 750, this discrepancy may be a result of the problem of access to water resources.

A second reason for the discrepancy is that all four types of resources (floral standing crop, floral productivity, vertebrate standing crop, and invertebrate standing crop) are not equivalently ordered by size across the microhabitats. For example, although microhabitat VI has the second highest floral standing crop, it is tied with microhabitat III for the third highest vertebrate standing crop. Table 5.3 shows the cross-zonal ranking by size of the four types of resources.

Table 5.3.   Cross-zonal ranking of resources.

Standing crops	Microhabitats					
	I	II	III	IV	V	VI
Floral	1	4	5	6	3	2
Floral productivity	4	3	2	5	6	1
Vertebrate	3.5	3.5	1.5	5.5	5.5	1.5
Invertebrate	3.5	3.5	1.5	5.5	5.5	1.5

The rankings range from 1, the largest biomass, to 6, the smallest. In cases of equal biomasses the ranks have been averaged. Computing Kendall's rank concordance[1] for nonparametric data on the four types of resources above, one finds a correlation of .72 which is significant at the .01 level and which explains approximately 50% of variance. Since 1.0 is perfect correlation, this indicates a good but not perfect homogeneity in the importance of the system's cross-zonal resources.

The question is whether the site distribution reflects a particular resource, a combination of resources, or the entire set of four resources. To determine this, the ranked site distribution was correlated with all possible combinations of resources. Table 5.4 shows the resulting correlation coefficients by "site-resource" combination. The number of sites was ranked by microhabitat at the time period of maximal resources and population. Two sets of resource ranking were used: one was based on the biomass figures; the other on the biomass adjusted by area. Kendall's rank concordance was used as the primary correlating technique, since it allows one to correlate any number of variables simul-

[1] See John Freund, *Modern Elementary Statistics*, Englewood Cliffs, Prentice Hall, 1960 and *Mathematical Statistics*, Englewood Cliffs, Prentice Hall, 1971.

Table 5.4.   The cross-zonal relationship between the ranked site distribution and types of resources.

	Kendall's concordance resources not areally adjusted	Kendall's concordance resources areally adjusted	Spearman's rho resources not areally adjusted	Spearman's rho resources areally adjusted
Sites and a single resource				
Sites and floral standing crop	.51	.74	.09	.49
Sites and floral productivity	.74	.80	.48	.60
Sites and vertebrate standing crop	.91	.89	.39	.77
Sites and invertebrate standing crop	.91	.80	.39	.60
Sites and two resources				
Sites, floral standing crop and floral productivity	.49	.61		
Sites, floral standing crop and vertebrate standing crop	.47	.67		
Sites, floral standing crop and invertebrate standing crop	.47	.68		
Sites, floral productivity and vertebrate standing crop	.52	.75		
Sites, floral productivity and invertebrate standing crop	.52	.80		
Sites, vertebrate standing crop and invertebrate standing crop	.67	.72		
Sites and three resources				
Sites, floral standing crop, floral productivity, and vertebrate standing crop	.52	.59		
Sites, floral standing crop, floral productivity, and invertebrate standing crop	.52	.65		
Sites, floral standing crop, vertebrate standing crop, and invertebrate standing crop	.51	.62		
Sites, floral productivity, vertebrate standing crop, and invertebrate standing crop	.71	.71		
Sites and four resources				
Sites, floral standing crop, floral productivity, vertebrate standing crop, invertebrate standing crop	.68	.61		

taneously. One needs to make no assumptions about the distribution, and the use of coded rankings circumvents the problems of unit equality. An italic coefficient is significant at the .05 level and a bold coefficient is significant at the .01 level. Spearman's rho for two variables[2] was also calculated in those problematic cross-zonal relationships where the number of cases is small.

[2] Ibid.

An examination of the significant correlation coefficients *shows that the highest correlation is between sites, floral productivity, and invertebrate standing crop.* If one considers all the significant correlation coefficients above .70, the floral standing crop is never a resource variable. On the basis of Table 5.4 it would be fair to say that the population distribution appears to be reflecting the floral productivity and the vertebrate and invertebrate standing crop.

Before the discussion of the tests of the first hypothesis, it should be noted under what conditions the expected rankings and the observed rankings would be similar. If consumption remained at 5% for all the microhabitats except microhabitat I where it dropped to 2%, then the expected and observed would be the same. This could be a result of the difficulty in getting access to the resources in microhabitat I which is 500 feet above the valley floor.

In summary, the data support the first hypothesis in both tests. In the first test the actual curves followed the predicted curves with the predicted relationship between the optimal and marginal zones. In the second test, although the zonal ordering of the expected and actual population was not similar, there was only a discrepancy for one microhabitat which could be corrected by decreased consumption ratio of 3%.

SECOND HYPOTHESIS

The probability for the second hypothesis being tested positively increases since the first hypothesis has been supported. The second hypothesis states that during periods of resource depletion there will be population aggregation. Although this hypothesis has been formally deduced in Chapter Three it may be worthwhile to conceptualize this process. First, the population is above the carrying capacity point or at carrying capacity when the resource curves begin to drop. Second, if access to resources is related to population size, then one would expect the smaller villages to be depopulated first. This does not have to be the actual carrying capacity, but could be the utilizable carrying capacity or the net societal product.

For example, let us imagine three villages, one with a population of 100, one with a population of 40, and one with a population of 20. If there is a 50% decrease in resources which results in a population loss of 50%, the three villages would then have populations of 50, 20, and 10. A second 50% decrease in resources would result in populations of 25, 10, and 5 (an average of 13.3 per village). The smallest village might not have sufficient manpower to continue its subsistence, religious, and political activities—its functions as a village. Thus, the smallest population(s) would migrate either to one of the other villages or out of the area of study. If the population migrated to another village there would be an average of 20 people per site. The point to be noted here is that if small villages continue, the number of people per village is smaller than if they do not (13.3 to 20.0). Thus, in general as resources decrease there will be fewer sites, but *relatively* more people living in each site as the small villages become extinct.

This hypothesis was tested using the 100% central survey data; results appear in Figure 5.3. The bar graphs represent the pinyon pollen which is the previously discussed indirect index of resources. The line is the average number of rooms per site which is an index of population aggregation. During the major period of resource depletion, from A.D. 1150 on, the number of rooms per site increases and then remains quite high. This indicates that during this period there is a population aggregation. This conclusion is justified since the effect of the smaller sites which would have lowered the average number of rooms per site is not exhibited.

After this hypothesis was formally deduced in Chapter Three, two additional concepts became relevant. First, it was necessary to assume for the formal deduction of the hypothesis that the rate of population change, *ra,* was greater than the rate of settlement change, *rb.* Second, if one relaxes two propositions of the deduction by allowing them to alternate with two inverse propositions, the deduction generates a more generalized hypothesis. That is, one allows the following propositions to alternate with each other.

4. Resources at time 1 are greater than resources at time 2. $R(t_1) > R(t_2)$

4a. Resources at time 1 are less than resources at time 2. $R(t_1) < R(t_2)$

6. The rate of population change is greater than the rate of settlement change. $(ra > rb)$

6a. The rate of population change is less than the rate of settlement change. $(ra < rb)$

Then, the deduction will show that population aggregation is an inverse function of resources.

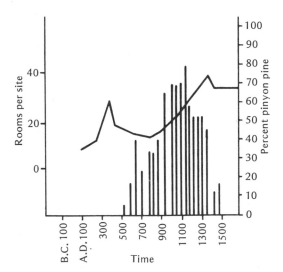

FIGURE 5.3 Pinyon pine pollen and the average number of rooms per site in the 100% sample.

Figure 5.4 shows the relationship between the climatic index and all the New Survey habitation sites in the 100% central and both 25% peripheral surveys. It is interesting to note how similar are the shapes of the average-rooms-per-site curves in Figure 5.3 and Figure 5.4. Figure 5.4 supports the hypothesis for the same reasons that were mentioned above with regard to Figure 5.3. Since the original hypothesis requires that the rate of population change, *ra*, be greater than the rate of settlement change, *rb*, during the resource depletion, the average *ra* and *rb* values were calculated for the post-A.D. 1100 period, giving the rate of population change = .49 and the rate of settlement change = .37. This is the exact relationship which is necessary for the hypothesis to be valid.

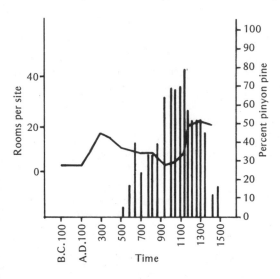

FIGURE 5.4 Pinyon pine pollen and average number of rooms per site in the 100% sample and both 25% samples.

Turning to the more generalized hypothesis which states that population aggregation is an inverse function of resources, one would expect the relationship to be similar to the one illustrated in Figure 5.5. This could be labeled the predicted relationship for the generalized hypothesis. The two variables are an index of resources, the percentage of pinyon pine, and an index of population aggregation, the average number of rooms per site. If one compares Figures 5.4 (data), 5.5 (the predicted relationship), and 5.6 (the actual relationship) the diagrams are similar but are not perfectly isomorphic. This is partially due to the fact that the resource data are limited and do not exist for the period prior to A.D. 500. Secondly, there seems to be a time-lag factor between A.D. 900-1100, where there is a minor increase in average rooms per site when there should be a decrease. However, the reality of the inverse relationship is indicated by findings covering the period from A.D. 1100-1300, when the resource index drops from above 80% to below 50%. This is also the period when the average number of rooms per site increases from 8.9 to 22.7. See Figure 5.4.

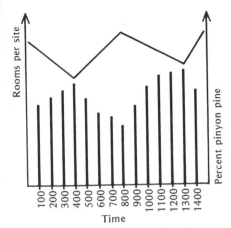

FIGURE 5.5   The predicted relationship for the generalized hypothesis between pinyon pine pollen, an indirect index of resources, and the average number of rooms per site.

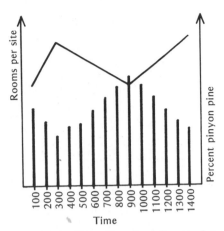

FIGURE 5.6   The adjusted relationship for the generalized hypothesis between pinyon pine pollen and the average number of rooms, showing the time-lag factor.

Figure 5.7 provides a comparison of the rate of population change, ra, and the rate of settlement change, rb, values through time and is consistent with the generalized hypothesis. When the average number of rooms per site is increasing and resources are decreasing, the rate of population change should be greater than the rate of settlement change. When the average number of rooms per site is decreasing and the resources are increasing, the rate of settlement change should be greater than the rate of population change. Periods with increasing average number of rooms per site are A.D. 100-300 and A.D. 900-1300. Periods with decreasing average number of rooms per site are A.D. 300-900 and A.D. 1300-1400. See Table 5.5.

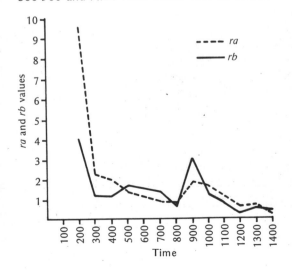

FIGURE 5.7 The values of ra and rb through time.

Table 5.5.   The survey *ra* and *rb* values.

Date	Expected	*ra*	*rb*
100-300	*ra* > *rb*	5.91	2.62
300-900	*ra* < *rb*	1.24	1.63
900-1300	*ra* > *rb*	1.01	.69
1300-1400	*ra* < *rb*	.21	.33

The information in Table 5.5 agrees with what is expected. Thus, it appears that although the resource data prior to A.D. 500 are nonexistent the data from A.D. 500 on support both the specific and general hypothesis.

THIRD HYPOTHESIS

The third hypothesis suggests that during periods of resource depletion there will be spatial aggregation. In other words, at the same periods of time that one notes population aggregation, one would expect to find spatial aggregation. This is the result of the increasing necessity for the population to utilize areas of optimal resource production during periods of resource depletion.

First, the habitation site and room densities were calculated as an index of spatial aggregation as suggested in the formal deduction of the hypothesis. Since the resource area is assumed to be constant over time, the rate of population change, *ra*, must be greater than the rate of resource area change, *rc*. Although the proposition base is met, Table 5.6 shows that after A.D. 1100, in all cases except one, the densities decrease. This indicates that the hypothesis is invalid using density as a measure of spatial aggregation.

However, as briefly mentioned in Chapter Three, density is not the most powerful tool with which to measure spatial aggregation. For example, imagine a square mile which contains five sites. If the five sites are within 50 yards or 500 yards of each other, the density will be equal, even though the former case shows far more spatial aggregation than does the latter case.

The nearest-neighbor statistic allows one to measure spatial aggregation whether or not the density is increasing or decreasing. Thus, the density turns out to be a crude measure of spatial aggregation when compared to the nearest-neighbor or mean-crowding statistics. Figure 5.8 presents the nearest-neighbor statistic[3] and the resource index, the percentage of pinyon pine. The curve is based on habitation sites in the 100% central survey area for habitation sites. However, nearest-neighbor analysis is invalid for discontinuous space. The two 25% peripheral surveys, of course, contain large quantities of discontinuous space.

---

[3]   Ibid.

Table 5.6.   Densities of the habitation sites and the number of rooms by microhabitat through time.

Date	I	II	III	IV	V	VI	Total area
Density of habitation sites—number of sites per square mile							
100					.35		.05
200	.85			.70	.70		.21
300	1.71			.70	.70		.27
400	1.71	.93		.70	.35		.33
500	1.71	.93		.70	.35	.50	.60
600	1.71	.93		1.40	.35	1.08	.92
700		.93	1.08	2.10	.35	1.51	1.25
800		2.79	2.17	.70		1.51	1.08
900		3.26	11.96	2.10	.70	3.83	3.25
1000		2.36	10.87	3.50	.70	4.74	3.85
1100			10.87	4.20		3.43	3.04
1200				1.40		.81	.54
1300				.70		.50	.33
1400				.70		.10	.11
Density of habitation rooms—number of rooms per square mile							
100					1.41		.22
200	12.82			4.90	5.63		2.06
300	55.56			4.90	5.63		4.77
400	55.56	.93		4.90	4.25		4.66
500	55.56	.93		4.90	4.25	4.33	6.70
600	55.56	.93		15.38	4.25	6.15	8.79
700		3.26	9.78	32.87	4.25	8.27	8.52
800		2.79	16.30	17.48		10.38	8.08
900		6.98	45.65	26.57	3.17	16.73	14.60
1000		16.74	39.13	76.22	3.17	24.90	23.71
1100		15.81	39.13	61.54	.70	34.88	27.46
1200				2.80		29.74	16.22
1300				10.49		18.55	10.80
1400				10.49		2.62	2.22

The nearest-neighbor statistic is an index of the continuum between perfect spatial dispersion and aggregation. Perfect aggregation, a single settlement, is 0.0; while random distribution is 1.0 on the scale. From Figure 5.8 it is clear that after A.D. 700 the spatial relationship between the sites is one of aggregation whenever the pinyon pollen index is below 50%. Thus, the data show spatial aggregation not with increasing density as predicted, but with decreasing density.

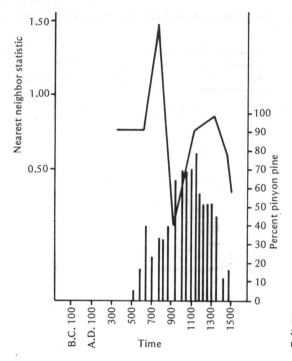

FIGURE 5.8 Pinyon pine pollen and the values of the nearest-neighbor statistic.

FOURTH HYPOTHESIS

The fourth hypothesis states that the residential area should also decrease during periods of resource depletion. The rationale behind this hypothesis is that whenever the population is above the resource curves there are insufficient resources to meet the demand. Until this demand is relaxed by out-migration or increased mortality, a set of resource priorities will need to be established. For example, under these nonrelaxed conditions a village should allocate more of its labor force to subsistence tasks than to the building of large residential structures. Thus, one would expect that residential area will decrease during periods of resource depletion due to the priority of the expenditure of resources on subsistence. Although it is possible that residential area would remain stable, the smaller replacement of outmoded or deteriorating structures would make stability improbable. The data in Figure 5.9 represent a sample of the 100% survey chosen by time and environmental zone. The resource curve is the same as the two previous diagrams. There is a close correlation between residential areas as measured by average room size and the resource curve. The results show a clear decrease in residential area as resources decrease, thus supporting the fourth hypothesis.

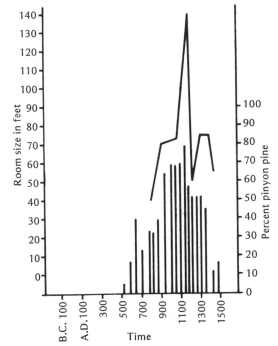

FIGURE 5.9 Pinyon pine pollen and the average room size.

The question with which this chapter began was to what extent do the data support the hypotheses? The answer is that the data support the four formally deduced hypotheses. However, it is important to note that although the data support the third hypothesis, it is necessary to use more refined measures of spatial aggregation than site density. The original "density"-based analysis provided a negative test of the hypothesis which proved erroneous when the more refined "nearest-neighbor" analysis was used.

6

THE SIMULATION MODEL

In this study a model of carrying capacity as a dynamic equilibrium system was developed from which hypotheses were deduced and tested positively with data from the field. It is possible to use the model in a second manner. Rather than develop hypotheses, one may use the theoretical formulations and the interrelationships of the variables stated by the propositions of the model to simulate reality. The comprehensive model has been further developed and has been rewritten as a simulation model. (See the flow chart of this model in Figure 2.19.)[1] The structure and general processes of the simulation model have been examined in the discussion of the comprehensive model. The simulation

---

[1] The listing and complete flow-charting of the program of the simulation model with summary documentation and explanation may be found in *Southwestern Test of an Anthropological Model of Population Dynamics* (Zubrow 1971).

is a restatement of the model in FORTRAN. By incorporating actual resource data and a variety of parameter estimates (such as birth and death rates), the simulation recreates through the model a series of villages. At each particular time interval these villages have a population, a location, a duration, and a subsistence area. The simulation also calculates the amount of migration between villages and zones, and when necessary, it creates or destroys villages. It follows the flow chart step by step.

Thus, to reiterate the process, the simulation originates with a small population in a single settlement. As time passes and ecological conditions change the population grows and a budding process results in new settlements. The growth process continues until the settlements reach a maximum population. As resources diminish, the populations diminish and the settlements aggregate. Finally, they become extinct. The population growth function determines, at different birth, death and migration rates, how much the population grows through a given time span. The population resource (net societal product) check defines the amount of resources which exist, the net societal product, and how much of the net societal product may be used at a particular level of technology (following Schumpeter), and checks the population size against these limiting values. The settlement locator determines which zone and where in each zone new settlements will exist. Finally, the longevity function determines how long each settlement will exist for nonresource reasons discussed above.

At the most simplistic level the four components fit together in the following way. The population growth component operates until the population resource check component shows that the population is too large for the zone. If it is not, the settlement locator locates a new settlement in the same zone as the original settlement and populates it with the excess population. If the total population is too large for the zone, the population resource check component calculates the best zone for the excess population, and the settlement locator locates the site within that zone. Finally, the longevity function is called into play. If it causes a population to become extinct at a particular time, it resets the population growth function, the population check, and the settlement locator so that the settlement no longer exists. When resources in terms of usable net societal product diminish, the four components act in reverse to minimize the loss.

Actually, the systemic simulation model is more complex for three reasons. First, when there are multiple settlements growing in multiple zones and being checked against multiple resource levels, the number of possible variations and optimizations increases extensively, if not geometrically. Second, the population growth component and the population resource check component are defined by multiple equations and are not just single relationships. Third, the settlement locator and the longevity function components are both testing three alternative methods of determining the settlement location and two alternative methods of determining settlement longevity.

THE MODIFICATION OF SPACE: THE SIMULATION MAP

The simulation makes use of the ecological map of the Hay Hollow Valley. This map is actually represented as a 25 x 25 matrix in the computer. A 625-square grid system was overlaid on the ecological map so that one boundary corresponded to the western segment of the county road. Each square of the grid system was labeled according to microhabitat. In cases of multiple micro-habitats in a particular grid square, the square was labeled with the predominant microhabitat. This 25 x 25 matrix is used in two ways in the model. First, the settlement locators assign sites to a unique square within the grid defined by the square's Cartesian coordinates. Second, the settlement locators use the microhabitat labels of the grid squares to determine the validity of the location of a potential "budded" settlement. In other words, it examines the microhabitat label of a new location. Then, a series of alternative decisions are made based on the priorities built into the system and the particular configuration of circumstances involved in the development of the newly budded settlement. For example, after a village is budded, the microhabitat in which it will be located will be decided upon on the basis of the best population-to-resource and net-societal-product ratio. If the settlement locator chooses a pair of coordinates whose label does not correspond to this microhabitat, it will recalculate a new pair of coordinates until the appropriate label match is reached.

The microhabitat distribution for the purposes of the simulation is shown in Figure 6.1. This simulation map is similar to but not exactly equivalent to the ecological map because (1) the borders of the microhabitats now correspond with the nearest grid square boundaries, (2) some of the area immediately next to the microhabitat boundaries, although labeled one microhabitat, may contain more than one microhabitat, and (3) the area which the simulated map covers is not the total area which the ecological map covers.

OPERATING CHARACTERISTICS

The simulation was run on a CDC 6400 computer eight times to examine some of the operating characteristics of the model. The values of the birth rate variables were set at 3.0 and 4.0[2] based on a theoretical 300% and 400% increase

---

[2] The choice of these particular values was partially determined by ethnographic analogy and partially by the archaeological record. After examining the range of values for birth, death, and migration rates which occur ethnographically and ethnohistorically in the Puebloan Southwest (Zubrow 1969), values within the range of variation for observed reality were chosen. For example, Zuni (the nearest Pueblo to the Hay Hollow Valley) shows net growth rates of 2.2 between 1760 and 1860 and 3.6 between 1860 and 1960. Acoma shows growth rates of −2.0 and 3.4 for the same periods (Zubrow 1969).

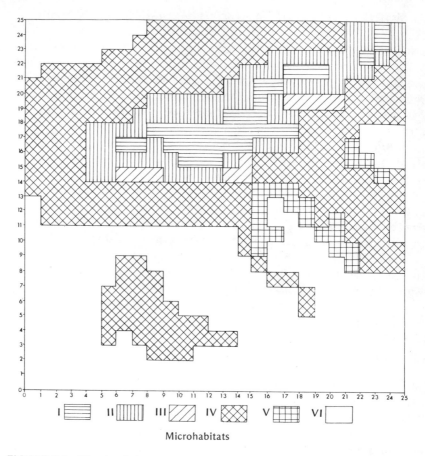

Microhabitats

FIGURE 6.1   The simulation map.

in the population per 100 years. The death rate was set at 1.5 or a theoretical 150% decrease in the population per 100 years. Theoretical values rather than actual values were used because other factors such as the availability of resources or migration will interfere. The migration velocity was given values of 1.0 and 2.0. Simulations which use the above variable values as well as the Mac-Arthur *tk* and the inductive probability longevity alternatives were run. The maximum settlement population was set at 400.

Table 6.1 shows the various combinations of values under which the simulation model was run. In all cases the simulation was begun at A.D. 200 with a single settlement of 50 persons located at coordinates (18,18) which correspond to a real site location with a settlement which existed at that time. The resources and net-societal-product values were based upon floral standing crop and productivity data discussed in Chapter Four.

Table 6.1.   The simulation: initial variable values.

Initial variables	Simulation							
	1	2	3	4	5	6	7	8
Birth rate	3.0	3.0	3.0	3.0	4.0	4.0	4.0	4.0
Death rate	1.5	1.5	1.5	1.5	1.5	1.5	1.5	1.5
Migration velocity	1.0	1.0	2.0	2.0	1.0	1.0	2.0	2.0
Longevity alternatives[a]	I	tk	I	tk	I	tk	I	tk
Settlement maximum	400	400	400	400	400	400	400	400
Resource growth	.05	.05	.05	.05	.05	.05	.05	.05
Consumption	.05	.05	.05	.05	.05	.05	.05	.05

[a] I = Inductive random longevity alternative; tk = MacArthur's tk longevity alternative.

Obviously, this series of simulation runs is not a complete analysis, but given the limitations of time and money, it was sufficient to demonstrate the heuristic value of the simulation model. For a more complete analysis, single and multiple initial villages located in all microhabitats in different locations should be used. Initial villages were those in existence at A.D. 200 when the simulation begins. Greater variation in the values of the birth, death, and migration velocity rates should be examined. There should also be simulation runs using different values of resource growth, consumptions, and settlement maximum, as well as floral and faunal standing crop and productivity figures used in various combinations and proportions.

For the purposes of this study we will present summary results rather than tables which trace the changing population of each settlement through time and through space as populations bud and contract in each of the eight simulations. Figure 6.2a-h shows the total population by microhabitat by time interval as generated by the various simulation runs. Figure 6.3a-h shows the total population and total number of sites by time period as generated by the simulations.

Several conclusions may be drawn from an examination of these summary figures. First, a birth rate of 3.0 produces a population peak or maximum population at approximately A.D. 1000 to A.D. 1100 (Figure 6.2a-d and Figure 6.3 a-d). A birth rate of 4.0 produces a much earlier large increase in population (Figure 6.2d-h and Figure 6.3d-h). The major period of increase is approximately A.D. 400-700. The population quickly reaches either its maximum or a high plateau value which it maintains until approximately A.D. 1100 with limited variations. Second, the earlier population increase and the longer maintenance of the larger population caused by the 4.0 birth rate occur both in the total population and the total population by microhabitat analyses. Third, the 4.0 birth rate is associated with an earlier development of population in the margin-

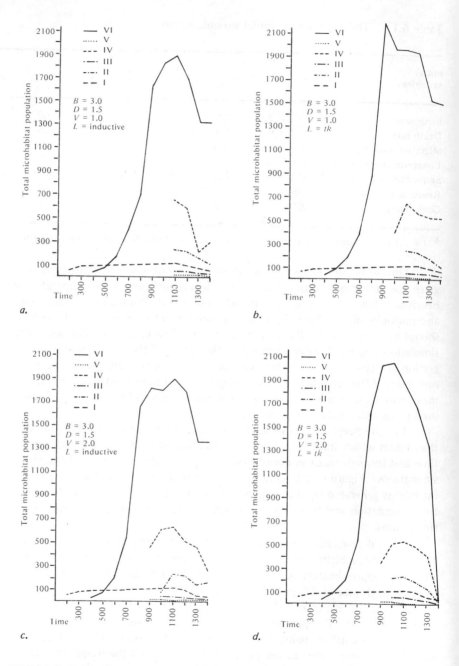

FIGURE 6.2 Simulations of the population distribution by microhabitat. The variables are B = birth rate, D = death rate, V = migration velocity and L = longevity alternative.

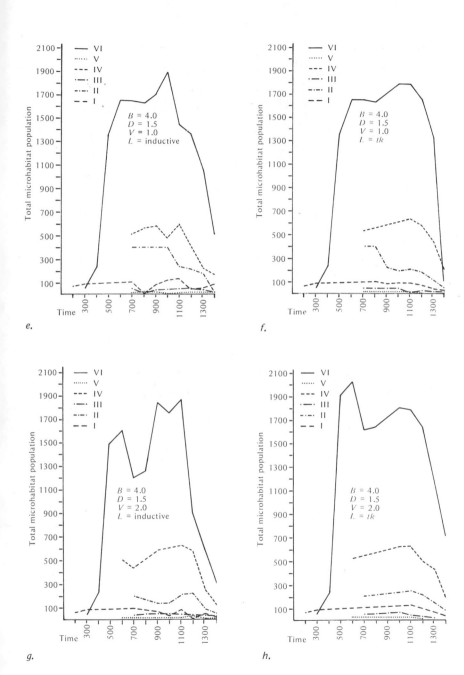

FIGURE 6.2 (continued).

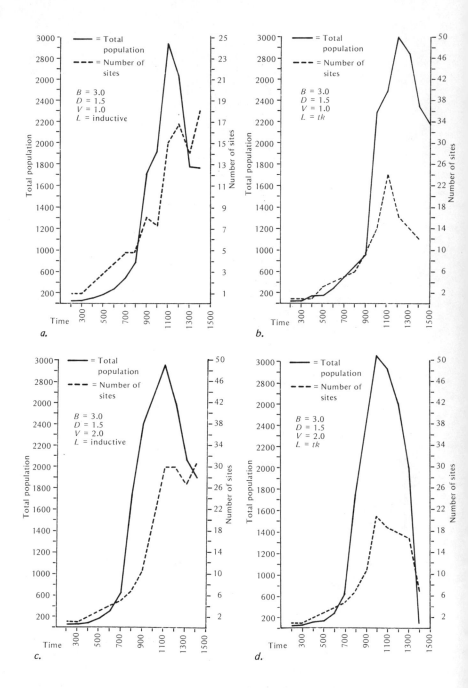

FIGURE 6.3 Simulations of the total population and total number of sites. The variables are *B* = birth rate *D* = death rate, *V* = migration velocity, and *L* = longevity alternative.

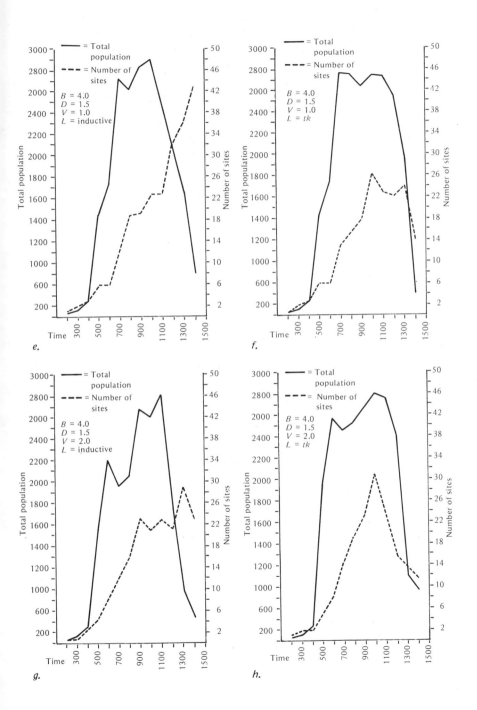

FIGURE 6.3 (continued).

al microhabitats. With a 4.0 birth rate the marginal microhabitats begin to fill at A.D. 600-700 (Figure 6.2d-h), with a 3.0 birth rate the marginal microhabitats begin to fill at A.D. 900-1100 (Figure 6.2a-d). However, the contraction of the population into the optimal zone takes place at approximately the same time (A.D. 1100) using either birth rate. Fourth, the 4.0 birth rate emphasizes the decrease in population which occurs after the A.D. 400-700 large increase in population (Figure 6.3d-h). Fifth, unexpectedly the 3.0 birth rate actually produces the largest population (Figure 6.3a-d). However, it is never sustained anywhere for nearly as long a time span as the 4.0 rate (Figure 6.3d-h). Thus, in overall effect through time the 4.0 rate results in a much larger sustained population. Sixth, if one compares the two longevity alternatives, MacArthur's *tk* results in a larger decrease in the number of settlements existing in the post A.D. 1100 period than does the random inductive longevity alternative (Figure 6.3a-d). Finally, the increased migration velocity of 2.0 usually brings population into one or two of the marginal zones a century or two earlier than does a migration velocity of 1.0 (Figure 6.2a-d).

It should be noted that in synergistic models such as the simulation model it is not actually appropriate to ascribe the causes of the above generalizations to changes in single variables, but to ascribe these causes to the changes in single variables acting in conjunction with other variables which remain the same.

One generalization about the settlement locators may be made before comparing the simulated settlement locations with the observed archaeological record. The program repeats the randomly determined coordinates of the village if the population weighted Bachi mean coordinates are located in a nonappropriate microhabitat. The vast majority of the weighted Bachi mean coordinates were located in nonappropriate microhabitats which indicates its lack of utility as a settlement locator.

THE SIMULATIONS AND THE ARCHAEOLOGICAL RECORD

Figure 6.4 shows the number of rooms in each microhabitat through time for the same area as was used in the simulation model. The data for this figure were derived from the total of archaeological surveys and excavations discussed in Chapter Four. Figure 6.5 shows the total number of rooms and the total number of sites for the same area.

Comparing these figures to the results of the simulation model (Figure 6.2a-d), one does not find perfect agreement between any one simulation and the archaeological record. However, all the simulations fit the archaeological record in respect to general configuration. One of the reasons that there is not perfect agreement is because the archaeological record is not complete. This is not to evoke the old "lost data" argument which states that since not everything is preserved, the archaeological record cannot be a data base for the testing of hypotheses or models. Instead, this does refer to the fact that part of

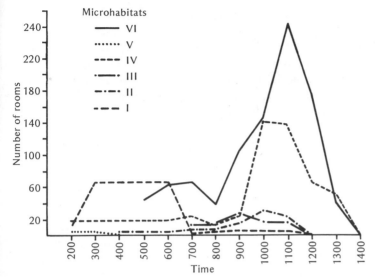

FIGURE 6.4 Total number of rooms by microhabitat from the actual area covered by the simulated map.

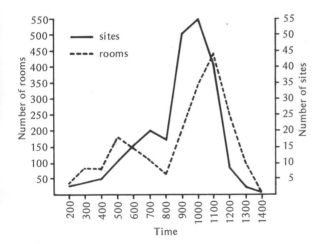

FIGURE 6.5 Total number of rooms and sites from the actual area covered by the simulated map.

the simulated area was only sampled and not totally surveyed. Since the samples were taken in such a way as to be representative, there is a very high probability that sites exist in the nonsampled area and which would, if known, change Figures 6.4 and 6.5. If, on the other hand, one used Figure 5.1, the number of rooms in the 100% sample, as a measure of the archaeological record, the two areas under consideration would not be exactly equal.

However, there are several interesting inferences which may be drawn from the comparison of the simulated expectation and the observed reality. It is clear that one gets a better fit in respect to the distribution of the microhabitat population with a 3.0 than a 4.0 birth rate. This holds whether one uses the 100% sample (Figure 5.1) or the archaeological record from the simulated area (Figure 6.4) as the measure of observed population. The population growth in microhabitat VI is not sufficiently sustained for a 4.0 growth rate. This lack of sustained population is also clear if one examines the simulated total number of rooms (Figure 6.3a-d) and compares them to the actual total number of rooms (Figure 6.5).

On the other hand, the observed archaeological record shows an early small-scale population movement into the marginal zones which better corresponds to a 4.0 birth rate. However, this could be just as easily explained by multiple initial settlements in different microhabitats, an alternative which was not simulated.

If one examines the population of each microhabitat, one notes that different birth and migration values and longevity alternatives fit together to come closest to the observed archaeological record. For example, microhabitat VI is simulated best by a birth rate of 3.0, a migration velocity of 1.0, and the inductive random longevity alternative, while microhabitat I is best matched by a birth rate of 4.0, a migration velocity of 1.0, and the inductive random longevity alternative. Similar results may be obtained by comparing the other microhabitats to the simulations.

This lack of identity in the initial variable values noted above is particularly interesting since it opens the possibility for different birth, death, and migration velocity rates, and longevity alternatives operating within each microhabitat or settlement. It is possible to isolate the factors even further. Once the microhabitats are filled, the model already readjusts the mortality rates and thus readjusts the net growth on a settlement by settlement basis. Thus, it is possible to conclude that the various microhabitats have differing growth and migration rates and longevity alternatives prior to microhabitat saturation.

Simulations run with more accurate adjustment of the variables as well as multiple initial settlements might show a higher degree of isomorphic comparison

One may consider Figure 6.2a as the "best" overall simulation if accuracy for largest proportion of the population is our criterion for "best" (Zubrow 1973). It most accurately portrays microhabitat VI, the optimal zone which contains the most population. If one converts the scales between Figure 6.2a and Figure 6.4, one finds that there are approximately 6-7 people per room. This compares with modern New Mexican Pueblos which have 1-11 persons per room (Zubrow 1969), and the Turner and Lofgren (1966) estimates for prehistoric and ethnohistoric periods, 5-7 persons per room. The simulated figures are obviously within the appropriate range of variation. They may actually be high because of unsampled sites which would increase the room count and thus decrease the person-to-person ratio.

Examining the settlement locators for the same simulation, one finds that approximately 50% of the locations are within the unsampled areas, approximately 35% of the sites are located where there are known sites, and 15% are located in areas where it is known that no sites exist. This supports the earlier conclusion that although the simulation estimates are probably high, they are in the appropriate range of variation.

CONCLUSIONS

It is clear that the simulation model essentially replicates the observed archaeological record. The basic configuration of population size, population growth, and the relationship of the microhabitat populations through time all substantiate it. In each simulation the population grows and as the resources and net-societal-product limits are reached, the marginal zones are filled. As the resources and net societal product diminish, the population contracts back into the optimal microhabitat. The status of the simulation mode, to use an analogy, is similar to that of a high quality stereo radio tuner. A station has been tuned in but the fine adjustment necessary for perfect stereophonic listening still needs to be done. The fine adjustment of the birth, death, and migration velocity variables, as well as the number of initial settlements and their locations and other variables, still need to be modified before one may expect perfect isomorphism between the simulation model and the archaeological record. There is some question of course, if the gain in knowledge is worth the effort of fine tuning (Zubrow 1973).

The operating characteristics of the system have been defined. Increased birth rates were shown to result not in larger populations, but in a large population being sustained for a longer period of time. It also results in an earlier expansion of the population into the marginal microhabitats as well as an emphasis in the decrease in population after the first major increase in population. MacArthur's *tk* longevity alternative results in a larger decrease in the number of settlements in the post A.D. 1100 period of population contraction and aggregation than does the inductive random longevity alternative. The increase in the natural migration velocity from 1.0 to 2.0 resulted in an earlier expansion into one or two of the marginal microhabitats.

The comparison of the simulations to the archaeological reality shows that although the processes are valid, there is the distinct possibility that each microhabitat may have different birth, death, and migration velocity values as well as longevity alternatives operating within its boundaries prior to the relative population saturation of each microhabitat. Finally, the simulation showed that the Bachi mean locator which maximizes population contact does not provide meaningful locations. However, the other two locators were twice as effective in placing sites where known sites exist in comparison to locations where there are no sites.

7

RETROSPECTIVE: POVERTY AND DEVELOPMENT

I began this book promising the reader that I would attempt to tread the fine line between a reasearch monograph and a textbook, to introduce the reader to some areas of research and how they came about, and to discuss some innovations in theory and methodology. It is difficult to write a conclusion without being redundant since each chapter has incorporated its conclusions as summaries. If this were a textbook, I could simply reiterate the conclusions or make suggestions for doing more advanced study with advanced texts. If it were a research monograph, I could conclude with the following statement: "A comprehensive theory of carrying capacity has been developed and shown to have analytical and operational utility. From the theory, hypotheses have been deduced and tested, a model generated and tested, and it has been shown that for 1400 years of cultural data the theory is explanatory." I could then point to further areas of productive research. Although both of the above might be sufficient I would prefer to broaden the scope of this conclusion and relate it more personally to my own viewpoint on the research.   **113**

One may ask why put such an effort into a theory which explains what happened a thousand years ago. For that matter, why should so much time, money, and energy be invested in a small marginal valley in Arizona which presently provides a livelihood for only six people. There are many rationales which could be developed, but here I wish to explore only one.

The theoretical problem raised by Malthus—the limitation of population by resources—and refined by the neo-Malthusians, has a philosophical import which is neither trivial nor resolved. It raises the problem of determinism. From the neo-Malthusian perspective human history is not the history of development and progress but the history of struggle and poverty. Man must struggle against the powerful four horsemen of the Apocalypse in the face of continuing diminishing resources per capita. Technical innovations bring respites. However, these are short term and are never allocated evenly across the population. Man's history is not the continual development of one innovation after another. Rather, it is the discontinuous development of innovations whose improvement each time are gradually being swallowed by increased population. Indeed, it is possible to argue that development and cultural change in the long run is the result of poverty and not the result of wealth. When a population grows until it can no longer support itself upon the existing resource base, migration to marginal areas takes place (hypothesis 1) and labor is reallocated from activities which are not directly subsistence-oriented, such as housing, to totally subsistence-oriented activities. This results in smaller residential areas (hypothesis 4), fewer villages (hypothesis 2) but larger populations (hypothesis 3)—the beginnings of sedentism. Rather than being a great step upward, this creation of sedentary villages locks the population far more tightly into a given area. It ends not with all of the population having a higher standard of living but with increased status differentiation. When parts of the population are no longer able to subsist on their plots of land, they sell their labor to the highest bidder, eventually giving themselves away in return for subsistence. Slavery, then, (real or economic) becomes institutionalized.

The reader will probably find this picture disturbing; I do. It contradicts three of the four underlying general tenets of western thought. This neo-Malthusian picture corresponds to the belief that there is an organization in the natural and social universe which scientific method can determine. But, this picture contrasts with the main tradition of our intellectual history in denying what is commonly called the "dignity of man." Human beings may not be treated as things or animals nor do they follow the same rules because they have "free choice," "souls," "liberty, equality, or fraternity." This picture rejects the notion of the "good life here on earth." It is expected that man will approach that golden mean between striving for the ideal, that unattainable goal, and hedonistic pleasure with its interests in the present world. Western thought has conceived of the social world from which it comes not as a uniform phenomenon but as a variegated set of experiences, social ties, and cultural groupings. Our cultural history is the history of persons, families, corporations, and nations. There is a place not only for group but for individual variation. It is not the grim uniform struggle for existence that underlies all neo-Malthusian models.

The battlelines, then, for a major problem are drawn. Rational, dignified (even pompous) man freely chooses his course of development from a variety of cultural forms or man, his dignity doubtful, rationality irrelevant, struggles with a series of inexorable principles which apply uniformly to societies without respite.

For over a thousand years these principles held up within one valley and I cannot say anything about the dignity or rationality of the inhabitants. These variables are more difficult to derive from the archaeological record. Sartre posed the existential situation. One imagines the last resistant of the last resistance movement saying "no" to his oppressors in some forsaken cell. Why? Because he is human and he has that liberty even though there is no hope of advantage and he is the last member of his cause. The neo-Malthusians, his unmasked oppressors, reply "so what." Whether he says yes or no the processes of history continue, for man must eat.

For over a thousand years people lived in the Hay Hollow Valley and the only traces of their existence are in the archaeological record as structures, artifacts, and clusterings of other types of archaeological materials. When small villages of pithouses were first being settled in the Hay Hollow Valley, Rome was falling. While Charlemagne was being crowned emperor, agriculture for the first time played a significant role in the valley economy. While Pope Urban II preached for crusades, the gradual withdrawal from the valley was taking place from large pueblos. As Lorenzo Medici took over the control of Florence and the humanistic foundations of the Renaissance were being printed on the first presses, the valley was abandoned. For me, there is no difference— these are records of man's existence. Without these records, from our perspective in time and space, they did not exist. Our challenge then is simply to record man's existence, for time is one of the few frontiers which remains.

APPENDIX I

THE DEFINITION OF THE MAJOR EQUATIONS AND CONSTANTS OF THE MODEL

The Definition of Equations for Resource and Population Curves

Population. Following Rogers (1968), one may define four elements of inter-regional population growth and distribution. These are the initial population, births, deaths, and net migration. Symbolically, it is expressed

$$w^{t+1} = w^t + b^t - d^t + n^t$$

where w^t is the population at time t, the initial population, b^t is the number of births between t and $t + 1$, d^t is the number of deaths between t and $t + 1$, and n^t is the number of net migrants between t and $t + 1$. The growth then is, **117**

$$w^{t+1} - w^t.$$

Or if one wants to determine the "growth multiplier," it is easily calculated. Since the above equation may be rewritten

$$w^{t+1} = w^t(1 + B - D + N)$$

where B is the birth rate, D the death rate, and N the net migration rate. The "growth multiplier" GM, is

$$GM + (1 + B - D + N).$$

Often B and D are combined to give a net nonmigratory growth rate, R,

$$R = B - D.$$

These are the factors that are combined to allow the quantification of the population curves of the graphical model or the calculation of growth in the systemi model.

These population growth curves are calculated per settlement per time unit. Then the settlements within a microhabitat are summed to give microhabitat totals. These in turn are summed to give the total population for the total region.

The nonmigratory growth rate, R, of known underdeveloped societies ranges from .002, prior to the agricultural revolution to .020 — .029 for modern agricultural underdeveloped societies. These figures are calculated by averaging societal R's. Birth rates range from .038 — .044 while death rates range from .010 — .022. The simulation model originates with $R = 1.5$ and runs to $R = 2.5$ per century, or approximately .020 to .040 per year.

In order to calculate migration, two types need to be differentiated. First, there is "naturally expected" migration which is a concomitant solely of the existence of other communities and which is in operation at all times. Second, there is migration which takes place as the result of a population surplus disequilibrium. This latter type operates discontinuously. In other words, naturally expected migration must be calculated for every time unit. However, the population surplus disequilibrium is calculated only when the population of a settlement is greater than the settlement threshold or the microhabitat population is greater than the microhabitat's resources. Different assumptions and equations are used to determine the different types of migrations.

"Naturally expected" migration is based upon the following assumptions which I believe are reasonable, (1) Goodrich (1936) has shown that areas of low standard of living and employment tend to be areas of net out-migration, while areas of high standard of living and employment tend to be areas of net in-migration. It is assumed that the general standard of living and employment rate of all the settlements, based upon social, occupational, technological, and ecological similarities, are broadly equal. (2) If two areas are in different economic regions, Folger (1953) has shown that the relationship between distance migrated and the number of migrants may be different from the relationship within an economically integrated area. (3) The rate of migration has been shown by Bogue and Hagood (1953) to vary with the type of community or origin and destination, the direction of migration, and the age and other characteristics of the migrant. Also, it is clear that a high proportion of all migration streams is a flow between communities of the same type, such as urban to urban, farm to farm (Bogue, Shryock, and Hoermann 1957). The settlements in the study area are assumed to be of the same order in terms of type of communities. (4) The size, direction, and net effects of migration streams are not invariable in time or place but are reasonably sensitive to social and economic changes occurring in the various communities of origin and destination (Bogue, Shryock, and Hoermann 1957). Yet, the regional pattern of net migration tends to remain constant for at least several decades reflecting the continued action of a set of redistributive forces (Shryock and Eldridge 1947). On the basis of these tested hypotheses, one may assume that major trends in migration pattern last for at least two or three decades.

Zipf (1949) has shown that the "naturally expected" amount of migration between any two settlements is directly proportional to the product of the population of the two settlements and inversely proportional to the distance between them, that is:

$$Z = k \, (P_1) \, (P_2)/d$$

where Z is the proportionality factor related to migration, P_1 and P_2 are the population of the settlements, d is the distance between them, and k is a constant.

Since 1949 very sophisticated "gravity models" have been developed upon Zipf's basic ideas and have been discussed by Isard and Bramhall (1960). Critical, however, to all of them is the constant k which must be determined inductively if one wishes to use the gravity model as a predictive device.

In a recent study (Bogue, Shryock, and Hoermann 1957), the concept of the rate of flow or velocity of the migration stream was defined. This is an abstract measure that takes neither the place of origin nor destination as a starting point for the same results are obtained whether one uses in-migration or out-migration rates. It is defined as

$$V = M/PO \times 100 \text{ or } V = M/PD \times 100$$

where V = the rate of flow of the migration stream, M = the number of migrants in the stream, PO = the population in the area of origin, PD = the population in the area of destination, and PT = the total population of all potential areas of destination including the area of origin. Unfortunately, streams of migration have not been calculated for ethnographic populations. Thus, I am forced to fall back on modern data to get a range for V. Analyzing urban, rural and rural non-farm streams of migration from 1935-40 in U.S. populations, Bogue, Shryock, and Hoermann found stream velocities ranging from 4.4 to 30.7 for the five year period. Net migration velocities range from .4–2.7. Given the velocity, it is possible to use these equations to determine the number of migrants accurately. The model was run with velocity rates from 2 to 3.

The second type of migration takes place when there is a population surplus disequilibrium. The migration size is equal to the surplus value if there is a location within a zone capable of carrying the new population as discussed previously. More specifically migration takes place when the following conditions are met:

1. If the population of a settlement is greater than the settlement threshold and if the net societal product for the zone is sufficiently greater than the total population to support the excess population from the settlement, the intra-zonal migration will be the size of the excess population.

2. If the population of a settlement is greater than the settlement threshold, but the difference between the net societal product and the total population of the zone is less than the excess population for the settlement, then, that proportion of the excess population which may be supported by the net societal product of the zone will be the intra-zonal migration. In addition, that proportion which cannot be supported will be examined in relationship to the possibility of being supported in other zones.

3. If the population total of zone is greater than the net societal product of the zone and there exists a zone in which the population is not only less than the net societal product but sufficiently less that it can support part or all of the excess population of the original zone, than, there will be interzonal migration of that part or all of the excess population that can be supported.

The equations defining this second type of migration are in simplified form as follows:

a. If $PT\ (J) < NSP\ (J)$ and if $P\ (I,J) > ST$, and if $NSP\ (J) - PT(J) > P\ (I,J) - ST$, then $M = P\ (I,J) - ST$: but if $NSP\ (J) - PT\ (J) < P\ (I,J) - ST$ then $M = NSP\ (J) - PT\ (J)$ and $P\ (I,J) - ST - M = F$ and F is checked as X in (b).

b. If $PT\ (J) > NSP\ (J)$ and $X = PT\ (J) - NSP\ (J)$ and there exists a different value of J where $PT\ (J) - NSP\ (J) > X$, then $M = PT\ (J) - NSP\ (J)$ where J has its original value.

In the above F, X = dummy variables, J = the zone, $PT\ (J)$ = the total population of the zone, $NSP\ (J)$ = the net societal product of the zone, and $P\ (I,J)$ = the population of the Ith settlement of zone J.

Resources. The equation defining resource growth is inductively derived and is thus very simple. *Res (J)* at time 2 = *Res (J)* (1.0 + *RG*) at time 1 where *RG* is the resource growth. The values and the spatial distributions of *Res (J)* are considerably more complex. They are discussed briefly here and at length in Chapter Three and Chapter Six.

Settlement location

The settlement location equations must be examined in two parts—the zonal location equations, and the intra-zonal settlement location equations. The zonal location equations are simply a series of checks between total zone populations, *PT (J)* and the zonal net societal product, *NSP (J)*. If there are sufficient resources in the zone in which the population disequilibrium takes place for a new settlement, the new settlement is located within that zone. If not, one calculates the zone which is best capable of supporting the new population. This is accomplished by the following set of FORTRAN equations (*POS* = Possible recipient zone),

POS (1) = PT (1)/$INSP$ (1)
POS (2) = PT (2)/$INSP$ (2)
POS (3) = PT (3)/$INSP$ (3)
POS (4) = PT (4)/$INSP$ (4)
POS (5) = PT (5)/$INSP$ (5)
POS (6) = PT (6)/$INSP$ (6)

$Z = AMINI$ (POS 1, POS 2, POS 3, POS 4, POS 5, POS 6)

if Z = POS 1   then $BEST$ = 1
    Z = POS 2 $BEST$ = 2
    Z = POS 3 $BEST$ = 3
    Z = POS 4 $BEST$ = 4
    Z = POS 5 $BEST$ = 5
    Z = POS 6 $BEST$ = 6

$J = BEST$

The variables are defined as above with *POS* 1-6, *Z*, and *BEST* as dummy variables. *AMINI* is a function which chooses the smallest of the variables within the parentheses.

Within the zone there are three alternative ways of calculating where the settlement is located as noted previously. First, there is simple random location. This is accomplished by setting the coordinates of the site *(X, Y)* equal to two random equations generated by a pseudo-random number generator. The FORTRAN numbers are $X = 10*RANF(0.0)$ and $Y = 10*RANF(0.0)$. These *X* and *Y* values are then checked in an internal reference table to determine whether or not they are actually in the appropriate zone. If not, new coordinates are generated.

Second, there is location which is based upon the optimization of the relationship of the new settlement's population with the other populations in the zone. This is defined as the population weighted "Bachi mean center of the distribution." Anthropomorphizing the concept, the question is what location would allow the population of the new settlement to be in contact with the greatest amount of population in other existing settlements within the zone by traveling the least distance. This is calculated by the following two equations:

$$XX = \frac{\sum\limits_{I=1}^{n} P(I,J)XX(I,J)}{PT(J)} \qquad\qquad YY = \frac{\sum\limits_{I=1}^{n} P(I,J)YY(I,J)}{PT(J)}$$

where XX and YY are the coordinates of the new settlement, $XX(I,J)$ and $YY(I,J)$ are the X and Y coordinates of each pre-existing settlement I within zone J, $P(I,J)$ is the population of the Ith settlement in zone J, $PT(J)$ is the total population of the zone J, and n is the number of settlements in each zone. If the Bachi mean location does not correspond to the appropriate zone (as determined by the internal reference table) for which it was calculated, one arbitrarily uses the randomly determined coordinates.

Third, there is new settlement location which is based upon the allocation of nonutilized resources. Each settlement which exists in the time span immediately prior to the new settlement is using a particular amount of resources which can be calculated in terms of area. Thus, in order to optimize settlement location with regard to nonutilized resources, one may calculate the areas which are necessary to support the other villages. After centering these areas around the villages, one randomly chooses a new location not in the areas. The same reference table constraints apply to these coordinates as in the first alternative. The equations which determine this alternative location are:

$$XXX = RANF\ (0.0)$$
$$YYY = RANF\ (0.0)$$
$$AREA = \left\{[2500 \cdot P(I,J)/(4 \cdot CON \cdot APROD(J)]\right\}$$
$$R = \sqrt{(AREA/6.283153)/292.6}$$
$$R = \sqrt{[XXX(I,J) - XXX]^2 + [YYY(I,J) - YYY]^2}\ ,$$

where XXX and YYY are the coordinates of the new village, $AREA$ = the area needed to support the population of a village, R = the radius of the area, $P(I,J)$ is the population of the Ith settlement in zone J, $APROD(J)$ is the productivity of the zone J, CON = the consumption constant and, $XXX(I,J)$, $YYY(I,J)$ are the locations of the previous settlements.

Longevity

Two alternative sets of equations determine nonresource settlement longevity. Similar to settlement location, the longevity function may be expressed stochastically by a random variable.

IAA = 10.RANF(0.)
If *IAA* = 1 then, *P (I,J)* = 0.

Since the pseudo-random number generator delivers a number between 0 and 1 with an approximately even distribution of digits, one may expect at any given time 1/10 of the settlements are becoming extinct, on the average, but which settlement and when is uniquely controlled by the random number generator.

The second alternative is based upon MacArthur's finite probability for every population at carrying capacity reaching extinction. The function is:

$$tk = [D/(2P(I,J)R^2)]e^{2P(I,J)\log B/D}$$

where *tk* = the time to extinction, *R* = the growth rate, *B* = the birth rate, *D* = the death rate, and *P (I, J)* = the population of the *I*th settlement in zone *J*. The limiting parameters on *tk* have a critical effect on its size. For example, if *B* = 1.1, *D* = 1.0, *P(I,J)* = 10, then *tk* = 13, but with the same *B* and *D*, if *P (I,J)* = 100, *tk* = 10,000. The function *tk* when graphed will generally follow the shape of Figure A-1. The take-off point is usually between *P (I,J)* = 100-200 which is small enough to be common in Southwestern archaeological and ethnohistoric settlements.

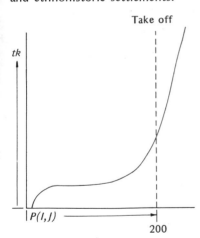

FIGURE A.1   MacArthur's *tk:* a longevity alternative.

Consumption Equations and Technological Innovation

The net societal product was defined as the summation of consumption, investment, and organizational expenditure. This is operationalized in the model by defining three variables: *CON, INV, ORG.* These are expressed as percentages and thus *NSP = RES (J) (CON + INV + ORG).*

There are only three major technological changes which have a significant Schumpeter cluster of innovations in the study area: (1) the development of agriculture which results in a resource surplus disequilibrium, (2) the development of irrigation which is also a cause of a resource surplus disequilibrium, (3) and the development of pueblo style architecture which results in, or is a factor in, a population surplus disequilibrium. The first two innovation cluster are self-obvious, but perhaps the last innovation cluster needs some further explication. Labor is a finite commodity related to population. Pueblo architecture takes a larger investment of labor than does pithouse architecture. This assumption is based upon the generally larger size of the pueblo as a habitation storage room combination, to the pithouse room. Secondly, since the population is considerably larger during the periods of time when the population was housed in pueblos, than during the periods of pithouse occupation, the amount of aggregate labor involved in architectural construction was probably larger. The allocation of labor is dependent upon societal priorities. If large quantities of labor are allocated to the production of architecture, less labor is available for subsistence activities, all other factors being equal. Thus, the innovations of pueblo architecture may be examined as a negative factor draining upon subsistence resources.

These Schumpeterian innovation clusters could be operationalized by a series of date-specific equations. At A.D. 700, the model would bring in agricultural innovations by increasing resources. This is accomplished by multiplying $RES (J)$ by a variable AG which is based on a combination of world survey agricultural figures (Odum 1953), Pueblo figures (Woodbury 1961), and ethnographic Hopi data (Stephen 1936). The equation would be $RES (J)$ at time 2 = $RES (J) (1 + AG)$ at time 1.

At A.D. 900 pueblo architecture would be brought into the model with $RES (J)$ at time 2 = $RES (J) (1 + ARCH)$ where $ARCH$ has a negative value. Similarly, irrigation would be brought in at A.D. 1000 with $RES (J)$ at time 2 = $RES (J) (1 + IRR)$.

APPENDIX II

The transformed statements of the hypotheses with their verbal equivalents are:

1. If the resources at time 3 are less than the resources at time 2 which are less than the resources at time 1, then the spatial development of the population in times 3 and 2 are a function of the spatial development of the population at time 1 and the total population. $R(t_3) < R(t_2) < R(t_1) \longrightarrow G(t_2) + G(t_3) = -G(t_1) + P(t)/A$

2. If the resources of zone 1 are greater than the resources of zone 2, then the population aggregate of 2 is greater than that of I, when the cross-zonal rate of population change is greater than the cross-zonal rate of settlement change. $R(J_1) > R(J_2) \longrightarrow PD(J_2) > PD(J_1)$

3. If the resources of zone 1 are greater than those of zone 2, then the spatial aggregation of settlements in zone 2 is greater than in zone 1 when the cross-zonal rate of population change is greater than the cross-zonal rate of resource change. $R(J_1) > R(J_2) \longrightarrow [P(J_1) /A(J_1)] > [P(J_2)/A(J_2)]$

4. If the resources of zone 1 are greater than those of zone 2, then the residential area of sites in zone 1 are greater than the residential area of sites in zone 2. $R(J_1) > R(J_2) \longrightarrow H(J_1) > H(J_2)$

The formal deductions for both sets of hypotheses are the same. Only the subscripts and spatial and temporal variables need to be transformed. As noted in the main text, what has been suggested is that if a hypothesis holds temporally, it should hold spatially and vice versa. If nothing else, it is a productive way to develop new hypotheses.

BIBLIOGRAPHY

Adams, John
    1966   Review of *The Conditions of Agricultural Growth: The Economics of Agrarian Change under Population Pressure.* by Edith Boserup. In *Annals of the American Academy* 367:224-225.

Ammerman, A.J., L.L. Cavalli-Sforza, and D.K. Wagner
    1973   "Towards the Estimation of Population Growth in Old World Prehistory." To be published.

Ashby, W.R.
    1968   "Principles of the Self-Organizing System." In *Modern Systems Research for the Behavioral Scientist,* edited by W. Buckley, pp. 108-123. Chicago: Aldine.

Bauer, Peter T. and Basil S. Yamey
    1957   *The Economics of Underdeveloped Countries.* Chicago: University of Chicago Press.

Berlin, Isiah
   1939   *Karl Marx.* Fair Lawn, N.J.: Oxford University Press.

Bertalanffy, Ludwig V.
   1968   "General Systems Theory: A Critical Review." In *Modern Systems Research for the Behavioral Scientist,* edited by W. Buckley, pp. 11-30. Chicago: Aldine.

Binford, Lewis
   1972   *An Archaeological Perspective.* New York: Seminar Press.

Birdsell, Joseph B.
   1953   "Some Environmental and Cultural Factors Influencing the Structuring of Australian Aboriginal Populations." *The American Naturalist Supplement* 87(834).

   1957   "Some Population Problems Involving Pleistocene Man." In *Population Studies: Animal Ecology and Demography,* edited by Katherine Breumer Warren, pp. 44-70. *Cold Spring Harbor Symposia on Quantitative Biology* 22.

Boas, Franz
   1911   *Mind of the Primitive.* New York: Macmillan.

   1938   *General Anthropology.* New York: Heath.

Bogue, D.J. and M.J. Hagood
   1953   "Subregional Migration in the United States, 1935-40." In *Differential Migration in the Corn and Cotton Belts,* Vol. 2. Scripps Foundation Studies in Population Distribution, No. 6. Oxford, Ohio.

Bogue, D.J., H.S. Shryock and S.A. Hoermann
   1957   "Subregional Migration in the United States, 1935-40." In *Streams of Migration,* Vol. 1. Scripps Foundation Studies in Population Distribution, No. 5. Oxford, Ohio.

Boserup, Edith
   1965   *The Conditions of Agricultural Growth.* Chicago: Aldine.

Boughey, Arthur S.
   1968   *Ecology of Populations.* New York: Macmillan.

Boulding, Kenneth E.
   1950   *A Reconstruction of Economics.* New York: John Wiley and Sons.

   1959   "Foreword." In *Population: The First Essay,* by T.R. Malthus, pp. v-xii. Ann Arbor: University of Michigan Press.

   1968   "General Systems Theory: The Skeleton of Science." In *Modern Systems Research for the Behavioral Scientist,* edited by W. Buckley, pp. 3-10. Chicago: Aldine.

Burkenroad, David
   1968   *Population Growth and Economic Change.* Unpublished. Vernon:
          Southwest Archaeological Expedition.

Butzer, Karl
   1964   *Environment and Archaeology: An Introduction to Pleistocene
          Geography.* Chicago: Aldine.

Carnerio, Robert
   1961   "Slash-and-Burn Cultivation Among the Kuikuru and its Implications
          for Cultural Development in the Amazon Basin." In *The Evolution
          of Horticulture Systems in Native South America, Causes and Con-
          sequences,* edited by Johannes Wilbert, pp. 47-67. Caracas: Antro-
          pologica Supplement, publication 2.

Christaller, Walter
   1966   *Central Places in Southern Germany.* Translated by Carlisle Baskin.
          Englewood Cliffs, N.J.: Prentice-Hall.

Cook, Thomas G.
   1970   *Social Groupings and Settlement Patterns in Basket Maker III.*
          Master's thesis, Department of Anthropology, University of Chicago.

Cowgill, Donald Olen
   1949   "The Theory of Population Growth Cycles." *American Journal of
          Sociology* 55:163-170.

Deetz, James and Edwin Dethlefson
   1965   "The Doppler Effect and Archaeology: A consideration of the
          spatial aspects of seriation." *Southwestern Journal of Anthropology.*
          21:196-206.

Dickenson, Robert E.
   1964   *City and Region: A Geographical Interpretation.* London: Rout-
          ledge and Kegan Paul, Ltd.

Domar, Esvey D.
   1957   *Essays in the Theory of Economic Growth.* Oxford: Oxford Univer-
          sity Press.

Dorn, Harold F.
   1950   "Pitfalls in Population Forecasts and Projections." *Journal of the
          American Statistical Association* 45(451):319.

Dozier, Edward P.
   1966   *Hano.* New York: Holt, Rinehart and Winston.

Duncan, Otis Dudley
   1959   "Human Ecology and Population Studies." In *The Study of Popu-
          lation,* edited by Otis Duncan and Philip Hauser, pp. 678-716. Chi-
          cago: University of Chicago Press.

Duncan, Otis Dudley and Philip H. Hauser (editors)
1959   *The Study of Population.* Chicago: University of Chicago Press.

Durkheim, Emile
1933   *Division of Labor in Society.* New York: Macmillan.

Ehrlich, Paul
1969   *The Population Bomb.* New York: Sierra Club and Ballantine Books.

Ehrlich, P.R. and L.C. Birch
1967   "The 'Balance of Nature' and 'Population Control'." *The American Naturalist* 101(918):97-107.

Einstein, Albert
1921   *Relativity: The Special and General Theory.* New York: Henry Holt and Company.

Eisenstadt, F.N. (editor)
1967   *The Decline of Empires.* Englewood Cliffs, N.J.: Prentice-Hall.

Folger, J.
1953   "Some Aspects of Migration in the Tennessee Valley." *American Sociological Review* 18:253-260.

Fortes, Meyer
1954   "A Demographic Field Study in Ashanti." In *Culture and Human Fertility,* edited by Frank Lorimer, pp. 255-338. Paris: UNESCO.

Freund, John
1960   *Modern Elementary Statistics.* Englewood Cliffs, N.J.: Prentice-Hall.

1971   *Mathematical Statistics.* Englewood Cliffs, N.J.: Prentice-Hall.

Fritts, H.C.
1965   "Tree-Ring Evidence for Climatic Changes in Western North America." *Monthly Weather Review* 93(7):421-433.

Gill, T.P.
1965   *The Doppler Effect: An Introduction to the Theory of the Effect.* Plainfield, N.J.: Logos Press.

Gini, C.
1930   "The Cyclical Rise and Fall of Population." Reprinted from *Population* by Harris Foundation Lectures. Chicago: University of Chicago Press.

Goodrich, C.
1936   *Migration and Economic Opportunity.* Philadelphia: University of Pennsylvania Press.

Gregory, David
  1969   *The Test of An Archaeological Hypothesis and its Possible Implica-
          tions for the Definition and Solution of the Problem of Urban Pov-
          erty.* Unpublished. Vernon: Southwest Archaeological Expedition.

Hagget, Peter
  1966   *Locational Analysis in Human Geography.* New York: St. Martin's
          Press.

Hairston, N.G., F.E. Smith, and L.B. Slobodkin
  1960   "Community Structure, Population Control, and Competition."
          The American Naturalist 194:421-425.

Hall, A.D. and R.E. Fagan
  1968   "Definition of System." In *Modern Systems Research for the Be-
          havioral Scientist,* edited by W. Buckley, pp. 81-82. Chicago: Al-
          dine.

Harner, Michael J.
  1970   "Population Pressure and the Social Evolution of Agriculturalists."
          Southwestern Journal of Anthropology 26(1):67-86.

Harris, Marvin
  1968   *The Rise of Anthropological Theory: A History of Theories of
          Culture.* New York: Thomas Y. Crowell.

Harrod, Roy F.
  1948   *Toward a Dynamic Economics.* London.

Heilbroner, Robert L.
  1961   *The Worldly Philosophers.* New York: Simon and Schuster.

  1962   *The Making of Economic Society.* Englewood Cliffs, N.J.: Prentice-
          Hall.

Hevly, Richard
  1964   *Pollen Analysis of Quaternary Archaeological and Lacustrine Sedi-
          ments from the Colorado Plateau.* Ph.D dissertation. Tucson:
          University of Arizona.

  1970   *Paleoecology of Archaeological Sites from East Central Arizona.*
          Unpublished. Flagstaff: Northern Arizona University.

Higgens, Benjamin
  1968   *Economic Development.* New York: W.W. Norton.

Hill, James N.
  1970   "Broken K Pueblo: Prehistoric Social Organization in the American
          Southwest." *Anthropological Papers,* No. 18. Tucson: University
          of Arizona Press.

Holdridge, L.R.
1947 "Determination of World Plant Formations from Simple Climatic Data." *Science* 105:367-368.

Isard, Walter
1960 *Methods of Regional Analysis: An Introduction to Regional Science.* New York: Technology Press of M.I.T.

Isard, Walter and David Bramhall
1960 "Gravity, Potential, and Spatial Interaction Models." In *Methods of Regional Analysis: An Introduction to Regional Science,* edited by Walter Isard, pp. 493-568. New York: Technology Press of M.I.T.

Johnson, John
1970 *Settlement Systems and Cultural Adaptation in the Hay Hollow Valley, A.D. 950-1100.* Unpublished. Vernon: Southwest Archaeological Expedition.

Johnston, Lewis F.
1966 "An Analysis of Sources of Information on the Population of the Navaho." *Bureau of American Ethnology Bulletin,* No. 197. Washington, D.C.

Keynes, John Maynard
1936 *The General Theory of Employment, Interest and Money.* New York: Harcourt, Brace and World.

King, Leslie J.
1969 *Statistical Analysis in Geography.* Englewood Cliffs, N.J.: Prentice-Hall.

Klein, Joel
1969 *The Alteration of Subsistence Strategies During Periods of Climatic Stress.* Unpublished. Vernon: Southwest Archaeological Expedition.

Kroeber, Alfred Louis
1939 *Cultural and Natural Areas of Native North America.* Berkeley: University of California Press.

Kroeber, A.L. and Clyde Kluckhohn
1952 "Culture: A Critical Review of Concepts and Determinants." *Papers of the Peabody Museum of Ethnology and Archaeology* 47 (1).

Kryzwicki, Ludwick
1934 *Primitive Society and Its Vital Statistics.* London: MacMillan.

Kuhn, Thomas S.
    1968   *The Structure of Scientific Revolution.* Chicago: University of
            Chicago Press.

Leone, Mark P.
    1968   *Economic Autonomy and Social Distance: Archaeological Evidence.*
            Ph.D Dissertation, Tucson: University of Arizona.

    1972   *Contemporary Archaeology.* Carbondale: Southern Illinois Univer-
            sity Press.

Lloyd, Monte
    1967   "Mean Crowding." *Journal of Animal Ecology* 36:1-30.

Longacre, William A.
    1964   "A Synthesis of Upper Little Colorado Prehistory, Eastern Arizona."
            In *Chapters in the Prehistory of Eastern Arizona II,* edited by Paul
            S. Martin and others. Chicago: Chicago Museum of Natural History.

    1970   "Archaeology as Anthropology: A Case Study." *Anthropological
            Papers,* No. 17. Tucson: University of Arizona Press.

Lorimer, Frank
    1954   *Culture and Human Fertility: A Study of the Relation of Cultural
            Conditions to Fertility in Non-Industrial and Transitional Societies.*
            Paris: UNESCO.

    1959   "The Development of Demography." In *The Study of Population,*
            edited by Otis Duncan and Philip Hauser, pp. 124-179. Chicago:
            University of Chicago Press.

    1963   "Dynamic Aspects of the Relation of Population to Economic De-
            velopment." In *Demographic Analysis,* edited by J.J. Spengler and
            C.L. Duncan. Glencoe: Free Press.

Lotka, A.J.
    1939   *Theorie analytique des associations biologiques.* Paris.

    1925   *Elements of Physical Biology.* Baltimore: Williams and Wilkins.

McKenzie, R.D.
    1968   *On Human Ecology.* Chicago: University of Chicago Press.

MacArthur, Robert and Joseph Connell
    1966   *Biology of Populations.* New York: John Wiley and Sons.

Malthus, Thomas Robert
    1803   *Essay on Population.* London: J. Johnson.

Marshall, Alfred
    1920   *Principles of Economics.* London: MacMillan.

Martin, Paul Schultz
>   1963   *The Last 10,000 years, A Fossil Pollen Record of the American Southwest.* Tucson: University of Arizona Press.

Martin, Paul S. and John Fritz
>   1966   Prehistoric Social Change in East Central Arizona. *Field Museum Bulletin,* Vol. 36. Chicago.

Martin, Paul S., John B. Rinaldo, William A. Longacre, Leslie G. Freeman, James Brown, Richard H. Hevly, and Maurice E. Cooley
>   1964   "Chapters in the Prehistory of Eastern Arizona, II." *Fieldiana: Anthropology,* Vol. 52. Chicago.

Marx, Karl
>   1909   *Capital.* Translated by E. Unterman. Chicago: C.H. Kerr. (Originally published in 1867.)

Mumford, Lewis
>   1961   *The City in History.* New York: Harcourt, Brace and World.

Murdock, W.W.
>   1966   "Community Structure, Population Control and Competition—A Critique." *The American Naturalist* 100:219-226.

Nagel, Ernest
>   1961   *The Structure of Science.* New York: Harcourt, Brace and World.

Notestein, F.K.
>   1945   "Population: The Long View." In *Food for the World,* edited by T.W. Schultz, pp. 36-57. Chicago: University of Chicago Press.

Odum, Eugene P.
>   1953   *Fundamentals of Ecology.* Philadelphia: W.B. Saunders Co.

>   1966   *Ecology.* New York: Holt, Rinehart, and Winston.

Paddock, William and Paul Paddock
>   1967   *Famine 1975.* Boston: Little Brown and Co.

Pearl, Raymond S.
>   1925   *The Biology of Population Growth.* New York: Alfred A. Knopf.

Plog, Fred
>   1969   *An Approach to the Study of Prehistoric Change.* Ph.D dissertation. University of Chicago, Department of Anthropology.

Ranis, Gustav
>   1963   "Allocation Criteria and Population Growth," *American Economic Review* 53(2):619-633.

Rappaport, Anatol and William J. Hovarth
    1968   "Thoughts on Organization Theory." In *Modern Systems Research for the Behavioral Scientist,* edited by W. Buckley, pp. 71-76. Chicago: Aldine.

Rathje, William L.
    1971   "Praise the Gods and Pass the Metates: A Hypothesis of the Development of Lowland Rainforest Civilizations in MesoAmerica." In *Contemporary Archaeology: A Guide to Theory and Contributions,* edited by Mark Leone. Carbondale: Southern Illinois Press.

Ricardo, David
    1911   *The Principles of Political Economy and Taxation.* London: J.M. Dent and Sons, Ltd.

Rivers, W.H.R. (editor)
    1922   "The Psychological Factor." In *Essays on the Depopulation of Melanesia,* pp. 84-113. Cambridge: The University Press.

Rogers, Andrei
    1968   *Matrix Analysis of Interregional Population Growth and Distribution.* Berkeley and Los Angeles: University of California Press.

Rostow, W.W.
    1962   *The Stages of Economic Growth: A Non-Communist Manifesto.* Cambridge: The University Press.

Samuelson, Paul A.
    1961   *Economics: An Introductory Analysis.* New York: McGraw-Hill.

Sax, Karl
    1955   *Standing Room Only.* Boston: Beacon Press.

Schiffer, Michael B.
    1968   *The Relationship Between Economic Diversity and Population Growth: The Test of An Hypothesis.* Unpublished. Vernon: Southwest Archaeological Expedition.

Schoenwetter, James and Alan E. Dittert, Jr.
    1968   "An Ecological Interpretation of Anasazi Settlement Patterns." In *Anthropological Archaeology in the Americas,* edited by Betty J. Meggers. Washington, D.C.: Anthropological Society of Washington.

Schumpeter, J.A.
    1911   *Theory of Economic Development.* Cambridge: Harvard Press.

Shryock, H.S. and H.T. Eldridge
    1947   "Internal Migration in Peace and War." *American Sociological Review* 12:27-39.

Simpson, George Gaylord
    1957   *Life: An Introduction to Biology.* New York: Harcourt, Brace and Co.

Slobodkin, L.B., F.E. Smith, and N.G. Hairston
    1967   "Regulation in Terrestrial Ecosystems and the Implied Balance of Nature" *The American Naturalist* 101(918):109-124.

Smith, Adam
    1937   *An Enquiry into the Nature and Causes of the Wealth of Nations.* New York: Modern Library. (Originally published in 1776.)

Smith, Robert L.
    1966   *Ecology and Field Biology.* New York: Harper and Row.

Spencer, H.
    1952   "A Theory of Population, Deduced from the General Laws of Animal Fertility." *Westminister Review* 57:468-501.

Spengler, Joseph
    1959   "Economics and Demography." In *The Study of Population,* edited by Phillip Hauser and Otis D. Duncan, pp. 791-831. Chicago: University of Chicago Press.

Stephen, Alexander M.
    1936   *Hope Journal.* New York: Columbia University Press.

Steward, Julian H.
    1949   "Cultural Causality and Law: A Trial Formulation of the Development of Early Civilizations." *American Anthropologist* 51:1-27.

Stott, D.H.
    1969   "Cultural and Natural Checks on Population Growth." In *Environment and Cultural Behavior,* edited by A.P. Vayda, pp. 90-120. New York: Natural History Press.

Sumner, William G. and Albert G. Keller
    1927   *The Science of Society.* New Haven: Yale University Press.

Taylor, W.W.
    1964   *A Study of Archaeology.* Carbondale: Southern Illinois Press.

Toynbee, Arnold J.
    1965   *A Study of History.* New York: Dell.

Turner, Christy G., II and Louvel Lofgren
    1966   "Household Size of Prehistoric Western Pueblo Indians." *Southwestern Journal of Anthropology* 22(2):117-132.

United Nations
  1953   *The Determinants and Consequences of Population Trends: A Summary of the Findings of Studies on the Relationships Between Population Changes and Economic and Social Conditions.* New York: United Nations.

  1955   *Processes and Problems of Industrialization in Underdeveloped Countries.* New York: United Nations.

U.S. Bureau of the Census
  1841-   *Nineteenth Census, 1960.* Washington, D.C.: Government Printing
  1960   Office.

Verhulst, P.F.
  1845   "Recherches mathematiques sur la lor d'acroissement de la population." In *Nouveaux memoirs de l'academie royale des sciences et belles-lettres de Bruxelles* XVIII:1-38.

Villee, Claude Alvin
  1962   *Biology.* Philadelphia: W.B. Saunders.

Watson, P.J., S. Le Blanc and C. Redman
  1971   *Explanation in Archaeology.* New York: Columbia University Press.

Watson, James
  1969   *The Double Helix.* New York: New American Library.

White, Leslie A.
  1959   *The Evolution of Culture: The Development of Civilization to the Fall of Rome.* New York: McGraw-Hill.

Willey, Gordon Randolph
  1966   *An Introduction to American Archaeology, Vol. 1. North and Middle America.* Englewood Cliffs, N.J.: Prentice-Hall.

Willey, Gordon Randolph and Philip Phillips
  1958   *Method and Theory in American Archaeology.* Chicago: University of Chicago Press.

Wissler, Clark
  1917   *The American Indian: An Introduction to the Anthropology of the New World.* New York: D.C. McMurtrie.

Wolf, Eric R.
  1966   *Peasants.* Englewood Cliffs, N.J.: Prentice-Hall.

Woodbury, Richard Benjamin
  1961   "Prehistoric Agriculture at Point of Pines, Arizona." *Society for American Archaeology*, Memoir No. 17. Salt Lake City.

Wrigley, E.A.
   1969   *Population and History.* New York: McGraw-Hill.

Wymore, A. Wayne
   1967   *A Mathematical Theory of Systems Engineering, The Elements.*
           New York: John A. Wiley.

Zanic, Thomas A.
   1968   *An Analysis of Pueblo Room Type Divisions.* Unpublished. Ver-
           non: Southwest Archaeological Expedition.

Zipf, G.R.
   1949   *Human Behavior and the Principle of Least Effort.* Cambridge:
           Addison-Wesley.

Zubrow, Ezra B.W.
   1969   *Population, Climate, and Contact in the New Mexican Pueblos.*
           Master's thesis. Tucson: University of Arizona.

   1971   "Carrying Capacity and Dynamic Equilibrium in the Prehistoric
           Southwest." *American Antiquity* 36(2):127-138.

   1972   "Environment, Subsistence, and Society: The Changing Archaeo-
           logical Perspective." In *Annual Review of Anthropology*, edited by
           Bernard Siegal. pp. 179-206. Annual Reviews, Inc.

   1973   "Adequacy Criteria and Prediction in Archaeological Models." In
           Research and Theory in Current Archaeology, edited by Charles
           Redman, pp. 234-260. New York: John Wiley and Sons.

   1974   *Population, Climate and Contact in the New Mexican Pueblos.* An-
           thropological Papers of the University of Arizona, No. 24.

INDEX

139